WEALTH
SUPREMACY

How the Extractive Economy and
the Biased Rules of Capitalism
Drive Today's Crises

MARJORIE KELLY

Berrett–Koehler Publishers, Inc.

Copyright © 2023 by Marjorie Kelly

All rights reserved. No part of this publication may be reproduced, distributed, or transmitted in any form or by any means, including photocopying, recording, or other electronic or mechanical methods, without the prior written permission of the publisher, except in the case of brief quotations embodied in critical reviews and certain other noncommercial uses permitted by copyright law. For permission requests, write to the publisher, addressed "Attention: Permissions Coordinator," at the address below.

Berrett-Koehler Publishers, Inc.
1333 Broadway, Suite 1000
Oakland, CA 94612-1921
Tel: (510) 817-2277
Fax: (510) 817-2278
www.bkconnection.com

ORDERING INFORMATION
Quantity sales. Special discounts are available on quantity purchases by corporations, associations, and others. For details, contact the "Special Sales Department" at the Berrett-Koehler address above.
Individual sales. Berrett-Koehler publications are available through most bookstores. They can also be ordered directly from Berrett-Koehler: Tel: (800) 929-2929; Fax: (802) 864-7626; www.bkconnection.com.
Orders for college textbook / course adoption use. Please contact Berrett-Koehler: Tel: (800) 929-2929; Fax: (802) 864-7626.

Distributed to the U.S. trade and internationally by Penguin Random House Publisher Services.

Berrett-Koehler and the BK logo are registered trademarks of Berrett-Koehler Publishers, Inc.

Printed in Canada

Berrett-Koehler books are printed on long-lasting acid-free paper. When it is available, we choose paper that has been manufactured by environmentally responsible processes. These may include using trees grown in sustainable forests, incorporating recycled paper, minimizing chlorine in bleaching, or recycling the energy produced at the paper mill.

Library of Congress Cataloging-in-Publication Data
Names: Kelly, Marjorie, 1953– author.
Title: Wealth supremacy : how the extractive economy and the biased rules
  of capitalism drive today's crises / Marjorie Kelly.
Description: First edition. | Oakland, CA : Berrett-Koehler Publishers,
  2023. | Includes bibliographical references and index.
Identifiers: LCCN 2023007147 (print) | LCCN 2023007148 (ebook) | ISBN
  9781523004775 (paperback) | ISBN 9781523004782 (pdf) | ISBN
  9781523004799 (epub) | ISBN 9781523004805 (audio)
Subjects: LCSH: Wealth—United States. | United States—Economic
  conditions. | Capitalism—United States. | Equality—United States. |
  Income distribution—United States.
Classification: LCC HB251 .K45 2023 (print) | LCC HB251 (ebook) | DDC
  330.1/6—dc23/eng/20230314
LC record available at https://lccn.loc.gov/2023007147
LC ebook record available at https://lccn.loc.gov/2023007148

First Edition
30 29 28 27 26 25 24 23   8 7 6 5 4 3 2 1

Book production: Happenstance Type-O-Rama
Cover design: Adam Johnson

For Valerie Kelly

Contents

Foreword

AS A LEADER IN philanthropy—a field born out of wealth accumulation on the backs of Black, Indigenous, and people of color communities—I've written that we can only heal from oppressive systems after we tell the full truth about how they are hurting us. In *Wealth Supremacy*, Marjorie Kelly is a truth-teller, showing how our system's bias toward wealth maximization is invisibly entrenched throughout our economy—from the design of corporate governance and the income statement to the practices of investing and the power of wealth over government.

Kelly writes from a storied career in sustainable business and finance, having begun decades ago as the cofounder of *Business Ethics* magazine with the aim of celebrating only good businesspeople and ethical investors whom she believed could change the world. But she came to see that voluntary efforts by individuals aren't enough, that the problems we face are systemic. She illustrates in this book how the machinations of the extractive system hurtle forward regardless of anyone's intention, harming communities of color, workers, and Mother Earth.

Wealth Supremacy makes visible what a colonized society considers "normal"—exploiting the many for the wealth of a few, rather than building real, shared abundance. I call this the *colonizer virus*, which divides, controls, and extracts to keep us all from thriving. This force driving our global economy will continue to cause deep harm until we commit to healing these systems. Together, we can embody a new way of using money—not as a tool to divide, control, and exploit, but as a force for connection, belonging, and healing. We can use money as medicine.

I am grateful to Marjorie Kelly for this offering, which can help us to heal. She not only names and reveals the sickness, the bias, at the heart of our current economic system, she helps readers find their place in the shared work to transform it. We all have a role to play in making things right; this is the heart of the Indigenous principle of All My Relations. We all need to heal. Our suffering is mutual, our healing is mutual, and our thriving is mutual. May we all reflect and act to uproot the systems that are hurting us so that all our communities can flourish.

—EDGAR VILLANUEVA, author of
Decolonizing Wealth; founder and principal
of the Decolonizing Wealth Project and
Liberated Capital

PART I

NAMING THE UNNAMED

*An era can be said to end when
its basic illusions are exhausted.*

—ARTHUR MILLER

WE CANNOT FIX A problem we cannot name. The hidden force driving many of the crises of our day is wealth supremacy—the bias that institutionalizes infinite extraction of wealth for the wealthy, even as this means stagnation or losses for many. Wealth supremacy in operation is capital bias—the root bias at the heart of the system of capitalism.

This system functions as a modern-day colonizing force. Today's empires are portfolios of assets. Their first myth is that they must limitlessly expand.

As a result of this expansion in recent decades, financial assets now vastly overshadow the real economy of jobs and income and spending, a state that economists call *financialization* and have long warned us about. It has created a social order where finance dominates the economy, politics, society, and, to a dangerous extent, the natural world.

The financialized economy helps to drive economic injustice, society-wide fragility, and planetary-scale crisis. Financial extraction is the source of expanding inequality, the force creating the growing desperation of the precariat. Finance is also in the process of absorbing the natural world as a new "asset class" of ecosystem services, with the aim of "creating" trillions in new wealth for the privileged few.

In a democratic society founded on the truth that all persons are created equal, we have permitted in our midst an economic system based on the directly contrary principle that wealthy persons matter more than others. Deserve greater rights. Justifiably wield greater power. Rightly enjoy greater voice. Are due greater deference. And possess a limitless right to extract from the rest of us.

Naming the problem is a place to begin. As more people today challenge the system's norms, we claim our power and erode the foundation on which bias stands: its cultural legitimacy. We unmask the hidden roots of crisis. We begin exposing the myths that keep us tethered to a system that has little investment in our lives, our liberty, or our pursuit of happiness.

Already the fundamentals of a new direction are emerging across the world—giving a foretaste of a new paradigm for organizing an economy, beyond corporate capitalism and state socialism. It is a system where the ethos of democracy is infused into the institutions and practices of the economy itself, a democratic economy designed not for the extraction of wealth but for the flourishing of life.

The well-being of society and the natural order will be starkly different, depending on which path we take in the coming years—continuing our capital-centric system or building the movement for system change that will advance a new paradigm, a democratic economy.

Amid the chaos and breakdown of our time, imagining such a thing as system change may seem daunting, overwhelming, impossible. It's not clear what it entails. And if we glimpse it, we don't believe it could ever happen.

This book invites us to relax. To begin by seeing. To name what's going on. See the simplicity of it. The enormity of it.

And to let that seeing guide us.

1

WHO WILL OWN THE EARTH?

Two Paths to Our Future

IN THE TINY TOWN OF CIBOLA, Arizona, home to three hundred people, a firm called Greenstone—a subsidiary of a subsidiary of the financial conglomerate MassMutual—quietly bought the rights to nearly all the town's water. Greenstone set out to sell that water to the highest bidder, shifting it away from the vital living use of agriculture and selling it to the Phoenix suburb of Queen Creek for purposes like filling backyard pools. As county supervisor Holly Irwin told a reporter, "They're going to make big bucks off the water, and who's going to suffer? It's the rural counties going up against big money."[1]

Not far away, in Colorado, the hedge fund Water Asset Management (WAM) has become one of the largest landholders in the Grand Valley west of Denver as a way of advancing its strategy of collecting water rights. The hedge fund is following this strategy at the same time the region is undertaking a review of how to manage the water of the Colorado River, now threatened by drought, with flows shrunken by 20 percent in twenty years. For the last century, management of the river's waters has been overseen by the Colorado River Compact, a government framework with its attendant slow-moving, democratic process of settling conflicts, struggling toward consensus and shared sacrifice through community and government negotiation.[2]

Will democracy remain in control? Or will the end run of fast-moving, aggressive capital turn our precious, diminishing water into a new object for financial extraction?

Who will own the water of the earth? Who should own and control the water systems of our communities? Whom do we trust to be in control in the world of ecological crises we're coming to live within?

With the advance of climate change, some of the most immediately catastrophic impacts are hitting fresh water, now seeing growing shortages sure to accelerate. In 2022, the water system of Jackson, Mississippi—the state's capital and largest city—utterly collapsed, leaving many homes with no running water.[3] Numberless catastrophes like these lie ahead as we move into a dramatically different future for fresh water than the stable world we've long known, as rising temperatures, drought, and torrential rains disrupt traditional levels and flows of this resource that every living being daily requires. The United Nations World Water Development Report projects that by 2050, some 6 billion people—more than half the global population—will suffer clean water scarcity.[4]

Business understands this frighteningly well. In May 2000 *Fortune* magazine observed: "Water promises to be to the 21st century what oil was to the 20th century: the precious commodity that determines the wealth of nations."[5]

This awareness has spurred the new wave of capture sweeping the American West, from the Rockies to Southern California, as investors like Greenstone search out and buy up precious water rights. In the eyes of big capital, water is an "undervalued asset."

Big capital doesn't ask who should own water. Finance functions today as a colonizing force, and the colonizer seeks to own everything. Capital's aim is to possess water as a new "asset class" it can monetize in the face of looming shortages. Matthew Diserio, WAM's cofounder and president, is frank about the ambition at work—though he speaks of it in the cloaked, technical language of finance. Water in the US is "the biggest emerging market on earth," he says. It's "a trillion-dollar market opportunity."[6]

Water as the Common Property of All

It is from the standpoint of the colonized that decolonization begins, wrote Frantz Fanon, author of *The Wretched of the Earth*. It begins with the impassioned claim that our needs and our view of the world are fundamentally different from that of the colonizer.[7] Water is a global commons, "the common property of all," says longtime water activist Maude Barlow. "Water belongs to the earth and all species." Access to clean, affordable water is a fundamental human right, she says, echoing the 2010 United Nations declaration that water is a human right essential to all human rights.[8] No one has the right to appropriate water for profit, Barlow maintains. "Water must be declared a public trust."[9]

It's remarkable how instinctively communities agree with this view. Even more remarkable is the fact of who actually owns the water systems of the US today: we do. Some 85 percent of Americans get their water from a local, publicly owned utility. Polls and referenda show we want to keep it that way.[10]

In the words of Arizona assemblywoman Regina Cobb, who represents Cibola, capital is trying to make water a commodity, but "that's not what water is meant to be."[11] There are towns—desperate for the income and investment—that have privatized their water systems, turning management or sometimes outright ownership of these systems over to private corporations. But often voters reject this approach. In places like Trenton, New Jersey, Baltimore, and Edison, New Jersey, voters massively rejected water privatization, with more than 75 percent voting against it.[12] Similarly in the UK, as Mary Grant of Food & Water Watch put it, "People feel deeply connected to water and that it needs to be in public and local control."[13]

Pause again to consider the fact that close to 85 percent of Americans get their water from a local, democratically owned and controlled utility. The largest is the municipally owned Los Angeles Department of Water and Power, which serves 4 million residents and businesses. This is a democratic economy already in operation. We the people *right now* own and control the water systems of American communities. And we are apparently enjoying superior service as a result, if the measure of success is something other than maximum profit for investors. While conclusive data isn't available, my former Democracy Collaborative colleague Thomas Hanna, who's now with the philanthropic organization Arnold Ventures, in a study found that privately owned water utilities in the US often charge consumers higher prices. He also cited concerns that private operators perform poorly and that their management leaves citizens uneasy with the lack of local, direct accountability.[14]

The Rising Wave of a Movement

Imagine you and I one day find ourselves in the position of those folks in Jackson, with no running water coming out of our taps. Who do we want to be calling? Massive absentee corporations with their robo-answering systems (staffed by hard-to-reach humans possibly in Delhi), or local managers accountable to the mayor and city council? Do we want to be paying reasonable or soaring rates?

In the UK since 1989, following privatization of water, water bills for customers climbed by one third. The water industry now boasts 32 percent profit margins. As private water companies paid out £72 billion in dividends to shareholders, sewage leaks fueled public rage. In the service area of the privately owned Thames Water, so much sewage built up in the River Thames that residents of Little Marlow started calling their part of the river "crappuccino." Sewage gushed into apartment windows in London. As activist organizations formed, the UK in recent times has seen the largest wave of protests since water was privatized three decades ago.[15]

The US is also seeing a rising number of antiprivatization organizations, with the growth of such groups as Friends of Locally Owned Water, Our Water Campaign, and Public Water Now. One crowdsourced study by the Transnational Institute and researchers at the University of Glasgow (Scotland) found seventy-two cases over the last two decades where water service in the US was returned to public ownership and control. Behind these shifts are often impassioned local campaigns. In Atlantic City, New Jersey, an antiprivatization campaign in 2017 was backed not only by a strong local alliance but also by forty state and national groups, including the NAACP, ACLU New Jersey, and the New Jersey AFL-CIO.[16]

Globally, a movement to reassert democratic control of water has enjoyed three hundred successful cases of remunicipalized water since 2000. One of the most delightful is in Paris, where the newly public water system installed water fountains around the city that dispensed *carbonated* water—"socialism with a sparkle," as Cat Hobbs with We Own It put it.[17]

This movement for local ownership and control of water is directly counter to the neoliberal revolution of Margaret Thatcher, who not only privatized the UK's water but also sold off gas and electric utilities, rail and bus lines, seaports, and airlines. In the process, she inadvertently demonstrated the superiority of local, democratic control of water—and by contrast, the debacle that results when private, profit-maximizing ownership moves in.

Still, big capital is out there on the move, backed by tens of billions in institutional investor capital, with many communities desperate for funding to upgrade aging infrastructure.

Which view will prevail? Water as a human right, a global commons? Or water as a trillion-dollar market opportunity?

2

TO FORM THAT MORE
PERFECT UNION

*From Extractive Capitalism
to a Democratic Economy*

IN THESE TWO PROFOUNDLY DIFFERENT PARADIGMS OF water, we can read alternate paths for our future, as we slide further on the downslope of ecological disruption. Which path we take will be a matter of which economic system dominates: extractive capitalism, manifest in models like hedge funds and multinational corporations; or a democratic economy, where ownership and control is rooted in community and embodied in various models (city-controlled water, worker-owned firms, depositor-owned credit unions, state-owned banks) which recognize our inescapable interdependence with one another—and hence the need for democratic accountability, for building economic pathways to form that more perfect union of a fully democratic society.

In the unfolding story of water, we can begin to see the architecture of economic system design. In one system, serving life is at the center. In the other, maximizing financial wealth is at the center.

At work in extractive capitalism is more than personal greed. It's a cultural worldview, a habit of mind, so pervasive as to be invisible. We can call it a bias, akin to race bias and sex bias, but toward capital and wealth, toward ensuring that economic activity is focused primarily on benefiting those who possess wealth.

It is in the nature of bias to be held unconsciously. To be seen as utterly normal. The executives and investors in the story of water capture likely aren't evil people, sitting about rubbing their hands like cartoon capitalists. They may be wholly unaware of the bias and privilege at work, much as whites tend to bear little awareness of the privilege that their skin color affords. If the effect of bias on others can be devastating—degraded water service, skyrocketing costs to consumers, sewage flowing into apartments—its presence in one's own heart is mostly quiet, unseen. Easy to miss.

When investors look at their/our portfolio returns, we step into the dreamworld of wealth, the fiction that financial gains somehow fall from the sky, pristine and unblemished. It is a world animated by the implicit assumption that capital interests are to be prioritized. That if the needs of others are ill-served by this mandate, it may be unfortunate, but income to investors must be maximized.

This is wealth supremacy. It's the bias toward wealth and capital interests that defines today's dominant political-economic system.

Like white supremacy, wealth supremacy is both entirely obvious and oddly hidden. How long had police been killing Black people during routine interactions before George Floyd? I lived in white Minneapolis and didn't see it, nor did millions of other white Americans.

In the same way, we see and don't see capital bias. Fully 71 percent of Americans say they think the system is rigged.[1] Yet few of us know *how* it's rigged. Its workings are veiled in the incantatory terms of finance (alpha, beta, ROI, IRR, EBITDA, ETFs). If most of us don't understand the system, those who do are too busy making money to challenge its norms. As Upton Sinclair deftly put it, "It is difficult to get a man to understand something, when his salary depends on his not understanding it."

Defining Wealth Supremacy and Capital Bias

Wealth supremacy is a manifestation of class bias. If class is many things—exquisite taste in art and wine, speaking and dressing well, having children attend the right schools—it stands on a foundation of wealth, which makes possible all the rites of class.

Wealth supremacy is about the many ways our culture favors the wealthy, the upper class. Much as history was once defined through the workings of great men, our capital-centric society defines the economy through the workings of great wealth and big capital. It's through the lens of capital—the operating face of wealth—that we define economic success: growing returns to investment portfolios, maximum profits, a rising stock market.

Wealth supremacy and capital bias are closely related, yet worth distinguishing.

Wealth supremacy can be defined as *the cultural and political processes and attitudes by which persons of wealth accumulate and maintain prestige, privileges, and power that others lack.* It's about status, in a culture where the wealthy are revered as the possessors of godlike powers. It's about influence, including the power to control philanthropy. It's about political and legal power—including the power to finance candidates, to influence lawmaking through lobbying, and to escape the justice system that ensnares those without wealth.

Capital bias encompasses areas most of us know less about. It's the face that wealth wears in the realm of corporations, investing, accounting, and trade—areas in which fewer are conversant. It's here that the real work of protecting and growing wealth is done.

Capital bias can be defined as *the bias toward the maximum increase of capital—maximum benefit to wealth holders—that operates inside the processes and institutions through which capital deploys functional power.* While *wealth* connotes a pile of dollars, euros, pounds sterling, or yen, *capital* connotes the active face of wealth. Capital is money that must limitlessly grow. It's the driver of wealth, operating through the mechanisms of profit extraction, the way accounting rules are defined, how speculation cloaks itself as investing—all the customs and rules by which wealth grows and is protected from loss and accountability.

Together, wealth supremacy and capital bias constitute the DNA of our capital-centric economic system. These entwined strands of bias define how the system talks, walks, grows limbs, expands, regenerates itself. The aim is to keep the wealthy on top, protected, comfortable. Bias toward capital is how that's accomplished. Capital bias *is* the system. It's a system of capital-ism.

Financial Overshoot and the Polycrisis

Today, as this system reaches its swollen, financialized apogee, its ongoing processes of wealth extraction have become the deep force sapping the resilience of our society, driving, exacerbating, or profiting from the largest crises of our day. Global systemic risks—climate change, biodiversity loss, deepening inequality, and rising authoritarianism—are converging into what's being called a *polycrisis*. While ecological overshoot is one root cause of this polycrisis, equally implicated is *financial overshoot*: the accumulation of too much financial wealth, even as the system remains intent on a limitless more.

The long rise of irresponsible consumption has been driven by the corporate drive to maximize profits. Our efforts to tackle climate change have been blocked by the misdirection of fossil fuel companies and the capture of politics by monied interests. As a global food crisis has unfolded, corporations have been out there using inflation to hide outsized price increases.[2] The white working class, left adrift by the loss of good jobs, finds its anger misdirected into racial and misogynistic hatred by the conservative forces determined to retain or reinstate the social order governed by wealth, by men, by whites.

Many of us don't fully grasp how the complex, obscure, mathematical rules and norms of our extractive system lie behind these crises. It's rarely explained to us how expanding pools of great wealth create and rely upon the precarity and indebtedness of the rest of us. Instead, our culture tends to view "wealth creation" as benign and wonderful.

This bias toward wealth makes it difficult for us to digest the warnings of economists that the world is awash in *far too much* financial capital, just as the atmosphere is awash in too much carbon.

At the level of the individual portfolio, maximizing gains makes sense—just as it makes sense, individually, to drive our fossil-fuel-consuming cars as much as we want and to set our thermostats as high as we want. But when we do so, in the aggregate we change the living function of the entire planet.

Similarly massive damage is created by financial extraction: a growing crisis of families trapped by predatory lending and unsustainable debt, the stifling of small and medium-size businesses that create jobs, dark money's attack on democracy. The deep, tectonic plates of society are stressed, overloaded by the accumulation of too much so-called wealth and the ongoing, expanding extraction it requires. But the language and myths of the system block us from grasping this. The very words we use reflect the view of wealth. More assets! How wonderful!

In reality, every asset held by one person is a claim against someone or something else. Debt is a claim on your income. A share of stock is a claim on a company's value, and boosting that value often means cutting workers' income to increase profits. In the case of UK water systems, it means raising prices on consumers so handsome dividends can be passed to shareholders. (Financialization is discussed more in chapters 7 and 11.)

If we spoke from the perspective of ordinary folks, we'd talk less about the stock market and more about jobs sent overseas and Uberized. Instead of celebrating great endowment returns, we'd be talking about private equity driving firms out of business, or tallying the number of people going bankrupt because of a medical emergency.

The aggregate level of financial assets today is obscenely overblown. It represents a massive ballooning since the time I was a kid in the 1950s, when financial assets in the US were roughly equal to GDP (Gross Domestic Product). Today, financial assets are an intolerable *five times* GDP (see figure 2.1).

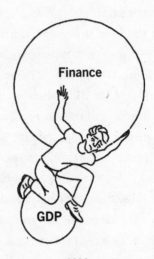

1950s:
US financial assets are equal to GDP

2022:
US financial assets swell to 5 times GDP

Source: Board of Governors of the Federal Reserve System

FIGURE 2.1: US financial assets are five times the size of GDP, a ballooning since the 1950s, when assets and GDP were roughly equal in size.

Society is like a household struggling under crushing debt. Yet that burden grows as financial assets grow, as wealth holders who hold economic power find more and better ways to extract from the rest of us. We're squeezed on one side by credit card debt, medical debt, college debt, second mortgages—and squeezed from the other side by low-income jobs, unstable part-time and contract work, rising costs, and unaffordable homes.

A once-functional system has turned treacherous. The wealthy are extracting massively from the rest of us. This is the problem we're not talking about yet.

There is a more democratic way to organize a modern economy. All over the world, there exist, right now, the hopeful, workable, saleable economic approaches we so desperately need to create stability and end economic injustice. Yet transformative change isn't taking hold at anything remotely near the scale required.

Instead, it's all poised to get worse.

The Foundation of Life as a New Asset Class

Consider how the two paradigms of economic system design—extractive capitalism versus a democratic economy—could unfold in our future, as we confront the question of who will own the earth, who will own and control "ecosystem services."

In one paradigm, Wall Street is laying plans to begin extracting wealth from ecosystem services through Natural Asset Companies (NACs), a new vehicle announced in 2021 by the New York Stock Exchange and Intrinsic Exchange Group. It's about "pioneering a new asset class," the sponsors said, which will capture and convert the productive value of natural assets like forests, water, coral reefs, and farms into investor returns. "Natural assets produce an estimated $125 trillion annually in global ecosystem services, such as carbon sequestration, biodiversity and clean water," the NYSE website exulted.[3]

Linger a moment over that extraordinary number: $125 *trillion*—the mouthwatering wealth extraction to be realized. For context, consider that the total value of the US stock market is $46 trillion.[4] That means so-called ecosystem services—the natural world, *life*—is "worth" *almost three times as much.*

Once you stop tearing your hair out, pause and note: if we think we've been colonized by capital, we haven't seen anything yet.

As progressive author and attorney Ellen Brown commented, NACs would make firms like State Street and BlackRock (and their multimillionaire investors) the "owners of the foundations of all life," permitting the extraction of incalculable profits.[5] Nearly limitless wealth.

"It's ludicrous," said Leslie Christian, when I called to get her view. She's the former CEO of Portfolio 21 Investments, where she cofounded an environmental mutual fund, and is now with NorthStar

Asset Management. "You'll have a private company allocating water the way they choose to allocate it," she said. It's about pricing resources high enough that people will conserve. "But that's a very high level, because rich people will pay a lot," she said. "You're depriving people of water if they can't afford it."

"Civilization is unraveling," Leslie continued. And this is our solution? Put a price on the essentials of life? "How do you value something without which you will die?"

There is another approach, proven to work. It is practiced in the hills of Luzon, the largest island in the Philippines, where the Indigenous community protects the forest. Called Batangan, it is a system of resource management built on a shared sense of responsibility for monitoring forests and planting new trees. It's also about "the water, the plants and the animals, the microorganisms," Victoria Tauli-Corpuz, an Indigenous rights activist from the region, told a reporter.[6]

This example was cited by a United Nations assessment on catastrophic biodiversity collapse that looked at how to ensure the one million wild plant and animal species at risk of extinction survive into future generations. The assessment was conducted by the Intergovernmental Science-Policy Platform on Biodiversity and Ecosystem Services, in which 139 countries participated. The UN report noted that Indigenous and local knowledge is crucial to sustainable use— and is at work in an estimated 15 percent of global forests, already managed by Indigenous and local communities.[7]

Hold onto that fact a moment: *15 percent* of forests are *already managed* by local and Indigenous power. This is not fringe stuff.

There are in reality two paths to the future. In Aldo Leopold's words, we can either continue seeing land as a "commodity belonging to us" or recognize it as a "community to which we belong." Humanity can remain in its role of "conqueror of the land-community" or realize we're a "plain member and citizen of it."[8]

Myths Obscure the System's Bias

One reason we fail to recognize the alternate path we might take is the system's uncanny talent for obscuring its true, brutal functioning. This is accomplished through a series of myths, which reassure us that the system's operations are purely mechanical, technically necessary, merely routine. Each myth is explored in its own chapter of part II.

There's the myth of maximizing—the notion that no amount of wealth is ever enough, a piece of insanity our culture sees as entirely normal which goes by the unexceptional name "return on investment." It's a process seen as ideally maximum, limitless, and perpetual, continuing even beyond death. This is the myth around which the entire system is organized.

Expanding wealth is a sacred obligation, according to the myth of fiduciary duty. So benign does this myth seem that we don't notice it's creating automatic and virtually universal protection for wealth holders, while leaving all others vulnerable.

A bizarre myth tells us societal and ecological damages are not real unless they impact capital. This is the myth of materiality, an abstruse concept in corporate and investment accounting that creates accountability to capital while rendering the rest of the world invisible and powerless.

There's the myth of the income statement: the belief that income to capital (delightfully named "profit") must be maximized, while income to labor (called by the horrid name "expense") must be minimized, a pervasive antiworker bias embedded in the conventional design of the income statement.

And there's the perverse myth of takings, the conservative worldview that tells us the first duty of government is to protect wealth, and that takings from the propertied elite are prohibited, yet that elite may take from others at will.

These myths and others embody the core narrative of capitalism, silently conveying to players in the system the basic rules, what is proper, how to conduct oneself. Such a narrative provides order, while invisibly crystallizing the idea that only wealth holders matter, that deferential treatment for the wealthy requires indifference to the rest of the world. The entire system's behavior is shaped—indeed, controlled—by this narrative and its implicit worldview, its bias.

That wealth supremacist bias, in essence, is the belief that those who hold wealth are superior, while everyone else is inferior. As Nancy McLean put it in *Democracy in Chains*, there are "those who ride and those who are the donkeys to be ridden."[9]

The Architecture of Economic System Design

We see in these myths the invisible way that a quiet, internal bias like wealth supremacy becomes a global system. The answer is system design. What is valued, who is valued, how those players are to be protected—all of this takes form in a set of simple elements that create the architecture of system design (see table 2.1). The democratic economy similarly has a design, shaped by the same elements but toward a different purpose, based on a different idea of who and what matters.

It begins with what we *revere*. One system reveres wealth. The other reveres life, the earth, our communities. Each paradigm carries an idea of who rightfully wields *ownership* and control—investors in hedge funds, or communities in control of forests. In one system, the *purpose* is maximizing income to capital. In the other, the purpose is enabling lives of dignity on a flourishing earth.

These systems deploy different kinds of *accountability*—fiduciary duty to investors, versus municipal utility managers with a duty to provide reliable water service at affordable cost. There's a necessity to report anything material to investors, versus concern for the actual material world of people and planet. Different conceptions of *rights* are at work—the right of corporations and investors to be free of democratic oversight in a "free market," or the human right to be free of unnecessary suffering, as with the right of access to clean water.

TABLE 2.1: The Architecture of System Design

DESIGN ELEMENTS	EXTRACTIVE CAPITALISM	DEMOCRATIC ECONOMY
Reverence	Wealth	Earth, community, democracy
Ownership	Concentrated ownership by wealthy	Broad ownership by ordinary people, public trusts
Purpose	Maximizing income to capital	Lives of dignity on flourishing earth
Accountability	Fiduciary duty to financial gains, rules of materiality	Duty of care for social, ecological, financial impact
Rights	Corporate, investor freedom	Human freedom, rights of nature
Governance	Stockholder governance	Democratic governance, stewardship
Infrastructure	Wall Street, central banks	Next system of capital

Governance is designed accordingly—investors alone having a vote for the boards of corporations, or worker-owned companies where workers vote for the board. Each paradigm is supported by overarching *infrastructures*—the infrastructure of conventional mutual funds and public stock markets, versus new funds and markets for local and impact investing.

Seeing these two system designs tells us something about why an economic revolution is not like a political revolution. It's not about replacing one leader with another (although that may be required). It's about *replacing one property paradigm with another.*

The Foundational Role of Property

Foundationally, system change involves a reimagining, redesigning, and reclaiming of our property regime, which has been colonized by big capital. French economist Thomas Piketty observed that every society has a *political regime* and a *property regime*.[10] Note he didn't say *economic* regime, but *property* regime. Regimes of ownership and control define an economy, for property is the base of economic power.[11]

In the millennia of agrarian society, kings and aristocrats worldwide owned the land that was the source of wealth and power. Under classical imperialism, entire nations—often nations of the "darker races," in W. E. B. Du Bois's terms—were turned into the overseas "possessions" of white European countries. As the industrial world expanded, wealth depended less "on the fortunes of harvests and seasons," as historian Eric Hobsbawm put it, and more on the fortunes of railroads, factories, and industry. These were owned by the railroad barons, the kings of industry, and their investors, possessing a new form of property: capital. In our financialized era, property has broadened again. Beyond land and factories, it now includes wealth from information and ideas ("intellectual property") and far more.[12]

Wealth is now thought of as *financial assets*. Property is represented as numbers. We think of financial capital as moving around in the blink of an eye, being invested, liquidated, harvested, ideally expanding without limit. The core purpose of our property regime remains what it was in predemocratic times: extraction of wealth to benefit a few.

Ownership as the Ground of Deep Transformation

Progressives don't customarily think of property and ownership as the ground of transformation. But it's the ground where what we value—sustainability, community, racial and gender inclusion—can find ultimate protection. It's where we begin the revolutionary work of establishing a democratic property regime—where the needs of ordinary people come before the needs of the wealthy, where protection of our common planetary life is a sacred duty, where difficult questions are resolved through hearing many voices. Where what is precious is legally protected and passed on to future generations.

Returning to the question of who owns the earth—who should own and control water and ecosystem services—there are some who might reasonably say, *Humans don't own the earth; we need to get beyond ownership entirely.* In this vein, Audre Lorde wrote, "The master's tools will never dismantle the master's house." Using such tools, she argued, we might beat him at his own game for a time, but we won't create genuine change. Certainly, it's true that simply shifting extractive ownership into the hands of the dispossessed isn't transformative. What's equally essential is *changing the nature of ownership itself*: from a right of maximum extraction to a duty of care.

So, no, we don't own the earth. We're called to be stewards of it, protecting it through vehicles like trusts and preserved areas, where life is not for sale. No one owns the fox. As Antonia Malchik, a theorist of the commons, puts it, the fox owns herself.[13]

Yet here's a vital point: when we do *not* create trusts, or public ownership, or other vehicles of democratic ownership, we leave what's precious open to seizure and plunder. We're defeated before we begin—as happened in America's internal colonization, when peoples who knew their ancient territories like the faces of their grandmothers were overmatched by a property regime that "divided the surface of the Earth into a standard unit that could be graded by quality, listed in ledgers," allowing land to be "bought and sold by bankers in New York and Boston who had never set foot on the land itself," as Claudio Saunt wrote in *Unworthy Republic*. A spiritual ethos of kinship was massacred by the extractive ownership mindset, which had at its heart, as Saunt put it, a "talent for abstracting the profits from the source."[14]

A Theory of System Change

When we begin to see that we have a choice—when we experience that dawning awareness that we can choose system change—we've begun to decolonize our minds. Inviting more and more of us into that awakening process is the aim of this book. A particular theory of system change is built into the shape of its flow.

Naming The first step in undermining the current system is seeing how bias lies at its very core. That means naming wealth supremacy and capital bias and learning to see their pervasiveness, which the book focuses on in part I.

Delegitimizing bias Seeing that bias is illegitimate follows naturally. This is the focus of part II, which exposes the absurdity and hypocrisy of the system by unmasking the myths that obscure how it privileges wealth. We will never win against extractive capitalism if it's a matter of power versus power. The real power we the people possess—the ultimate power—is legitimacy. When we withdraw legitimacy, we fatally weaken the system, turning its cultural foundation to sand.

Necessity Also vital is recognizing the necessity for deep change—not reform, but system change. This becomes devastatingly clear when we tally the countless damages wrought by financialization. Chapters 8–12 trace its calamitous results, such as the ruinous impact on workers, as capital drives labor income—and labor itself—out of the economy. Even more frightening is how the hard right, fueled by plutocratic dark money, now seeks to eradicate democracy in its quest to keep powering the machine that supports what Senator Sheldon Whitehouse calls the "unseen ruling class."[15]

Imagination If system change is unavoidably necessary, what other system is possible? Exploring this is the work of part III. The place to begin transformation is in our own minds, the one place the colonized are wholly free.

Demonstration Demonstrating the viability—indeed, superiority—of alternative models of ownership and control, as with community-managed forests and city-owned water, is where we see the imagined become reality, explored in chapter 16.

Pathways Laying pathways to expand democratic models, and to restrain financial extraction, is the way we tangibly advance. An undertheorized yet critical part of this is envisioning pathways toward an entire next system of capital, which is the work of chapter 17, based on a gathering of experts my colleagues and I convened. Together we envision a system where finance is democratized, where debts are forgiven when necessary, where disadvantaged children begin life with baby bonds, and where the apex predator of private equity is reined in.

What system change means is moving beyond the archaic conception of property and wealth privilege embodied in extractive capitalism. As Leopold remarked, our notion of property is "Abrahamic." It's of a piece with the patriarchal notion of dominion, the ancient paradigm of Western civilization where some are born to power and others to powerlessness, a world of us versus them, a worldview for which dominion by finance represents the zenith. Potentially a turning point.

The soul of the new paradigm is the coming of all into one fate. As ecological crises show us, we live in a world of interdependence—a world requiring reciprocity, as many Indigenous peoples have understood. If we're to survive here, writes Robin Wall Kimmerer in *Braiding Sweetgrass*, our work is to recognize the earth, its creatures, the land, as living beings. To see that the earth is sacred ground—a gift, not a commodity. To see others as our kin.[16]

The Seventh Fire

Systems outgrow their usefulness. They become hollowed-out, fragile structures vulnerable to collapse. Our own system keeps collapsing. We keep propping it up, because most of us don't yet dream of a next system.

Perhaps it's time we do so, as unlikely as such a dream feels, in this moment when the civility and security of our world is breaking down, when there's a sense that a way of life on this planet is ending.

We're in the time of the seventh fire, writes Kimmerer. For millennia humans lived "under the care of maples and birches, sturgeon and beaver, eagle and loon." Yet the cup of life now threatens to become the cup of grief. She writes of the native prophecy that at this time of great change, the people of the earth will stand at a crossroads, seeing that the path ahead divides. One road is soft and green with new grass. The other is ordinary pavement, deceptively smooth, but it buckles into jagged shards.[17]

The time of the seventh fire, the prophesy tells us, is a moment when a new people will emerge, sharing a sacred purpose. Sharing a great longing to live again in a world of community, a world of reverence for life—a different way of living together, already beginning to rise around us.[18]

And yet, at this same moment, that vastly larger wealth supremacist world we inhabit—faster, more powerful, absolutely sure of itself—is out there relentlessly seeking new assets for financial extraction: financializing housing, taking over swaths of the healthcare system, monetizing our identities, owning the gene code.

With the new asset class of NACs, the plan by Wall Street to monetize the foundations of life, I found myself curious how progressives were reacting. I searched the internet, expecting to find a swell of outrage. But it was pretty quiet out there, as this new form of colonization silently advanced. The idea of big capital owning trillions' worth of forests, water, farms, coral reefs—it seemed to strike people as pretty much business as usual. Utterly normal.

3

NAMING SHAPES REALITY

Wealth Supremacy and Capital Bias

THERE IS A LIBERATORY POWER in making the "unnameable nameable," poet Adrienne Rich wrote during her awakening as a feminist and lesbian.[1] Legal scholar Kimberlé Crenshaw, who co-created the concept of critical race theory, similarly said, "You cannot fix a problem you cannot name."[2]

Naming is a way of breaking the silences that enfold and entrap us, a way of shining light into the unseen ways that culture and language shape our way of seeing the world, rendering our very lives invisible, even to ourselves.

After a mass shooting of eight women—six of them Asian women—at Atlanta spas, Korean American minister Mihee Kim-Kort wrote, "To move through this world as an Asian who is American is to exist under the gaze of white supremacy." And to be an "Asian *woman* who is American," she continued, is to be "a ghost, invisible, unknowable, stripped of her identity," making her expendable.[3]

As Asian women exist under the gaze of white supremacy and male supremacy, our society exists under the gaze of wealth supremacy. The gaze of capital. This gaze silently encodes the message that the rest of reality—including workers (most human beings), communities (our cities, our nations), small businesses (the engines of job growth), and the environment (the planet, the ground of all being)—is all implicitly secondary. Subordinate. Naturally without economic power. And that this arrangement is legitimate, normal, and necessary.

The gaze of wealth supremacy is about a particular "view from here," about how some are empowered as the subject of their reality, while others are the object of that gaze.

We see wealth supremacy and capital bias in the way that property rights are considered sacred and untouchable, while worker rights are constantly contested. We see these biases in the way that the impacts of corporations on society and the natural world are termed *externalities*, making the real world oddly external to what matters: abstract numbers in investment portfolios and financial statements.

We see capital bias in how monopolist Amazon takes 34 percent of every sale by small-business sellers on Amazon Marketplace, enriching billionaire Jeff Bezos and his investors while leaving family businesses to struggle. We unwittingly participate in this heist as we hold stock in Amazon, or in index funds holding Amazon, while the infrastructure we need to invest in local businesses simply isn't there.[4]

Naming Tells Us What Counts as Real

What we talk about, the words we use, what the culture fixes its gaze upon—these weave into the narrative where bias lives. Naming is "a culture's way of fixing what will actually count as reality," observed Deborah Cameron, a feminist scholar of linguistics.[5]

Claudio Saunt, in *Unworthy Republic*, writes of how the dispossession of American Indians was often historically referred to as "Indian removal," which obscured the coercion and violence involved. The settling of the West was wrapped in a narrative of "Manifest Destiny" and the "march of civilization," a heroic narrative that masked the atrocities at work. In writing his history from below, from the point of view of the dispossessed, Saunt deliberately chose words like "deportation," "expulsion," and "extermination."[6]

Language is a cultural construct. It not only underpins reality but shapes our perception of it. "Language is our means of classifying and ordering the world," Dale Spender observed in her 1980 classic, *Man Made Language*. "In its structure and in its use we bring our world into realization, and if it is inherently inaccurate, then we are misled."[7]

French psychoanalyst Jacques Lacan observed that language constitutes a "symbolic order," which serves as the foundation of culture. As we learn adult speech, we enter this symbolic order and take up our place in society. When language is biased—when we speak of the human race as "mankind," when language separates us into fabricated categories of "Blacks" and "whites," when it casts worker income as "expense" and capital income as "profit"—we enter a symbolic order that denigrates us, marginalizes us or others, and disparages what we wish to honor. When we try to speak of what we care about, we are forced into silence, anger, and euphemism.[8]

Worth and Worth-Less: Who Matters, Who Does Not

Capital bias is deeply encoded in the language of economic matters. As with racial and gender bias, such language tells us who and what matters, who is superior and who inferior. We speak of someone's "net worth," which tells us billionaires have more personal "worth" than "deadbeats," who are worth-less.

Having greater worth, the wealthy deserve more power—as in corporate governance, where those possessing greater wealth wield more votes, holding the power to select CEOs. We think of this as being about property rights. It is more accurately about property *privilege*. In its feudal meaning, *privileges* meant legal rights possessed by the aristocracy that were unavailable to others, like the right of an aristocratic hunting party to trample peasants' crops, while commoners were forbidden to hunt even on their own land.[9] Similarly, private equity has a right to hunt down and take over companies, trampling on workers' jobs.

Legal privileges and cultural veneration are granted today to the wealthy, while workers and the poor are culturally denigrated and powerless. Conservatives speak of "welfare queens," casting as cheaters those community members who need and deserve support. The economy, we're told, has "makers and takers," with the "makers" being business leaders and investors, the people who are said to create wealth. Our language obscures the fact that much of so-called investing is really extraction; it's really a form of taking, as when private equity "invests in"—takes over—firms, loads them with debt, and drives them into bankruptcy, taking from workers the income their labor created.

To fall behind on debt is seen as shameful in our society. Aggressive debt collectors feed this shame as they pressure people who cannot pay, even when the choice is between food and heat versus debt payments.

The world of work has for years been in massive crisis, embodied in wages essentially flat for decades, jobs sent overseas, unions eroded, and the very nature of stable work transformed into precarious work temping, working part-time or on contract, or getting by on shaky self-employment or gig work. These "contingent" workers, as measured in 2015 by the Government Accountability Office, amounted to a vast *40 percent of all workers*.[10] That count is outdated—the phenomenon overlooked—because we lack the reliable metrics of our economy to make precarity visible. Since 2015, the government has not conducted a regular annual tally of the contingent workforce.

Blaming the Victim

The crisis of work today isn't met with the kind of alarm that meets every crisis in the stock market. The state of work rears its head in cultural awareness only occasionally, under inconsistent names. It's reported like a series of fads, rather than through coverage offering granular, usable information. There was talk of how the COVID pandemic revealed the plight of underpaid, overstressed "essential workers," and later of how workers were leaving jobs in a "great resignation."

Before that, talk was of the "deaths of despair" discovered by Princeton economists Ann Case and Angus Deaton, who documented the rise of deaths from suicide and self-poisoning through drug and alcohol abuse among working-age men and women. Their research found that these deaths correlated most strongly not with poverty or even income inequality but with the steady deterioration in job opportunities.[11]

People want to be useful in society, to be contributors. Even in this moment of postwork dialogue, celebrating many other ways to create meaning in life, many of those unable to find reliable, family-supporting work find their situation painful. In despair, feeling worthless, some seek to kill or poison their worth-less selves. When we lack good work, we lack standing in society, and we blame ourselves. When our life isn't going well, American culture judges us harshly.[12]

The public discourse too often blames the victims. If people are unemployed, they should fix themselves through retraining.

This view overlooks how our system of wealth supremacy works methodically against labor, as it works for capital. Society too often fails to acknowledge how capital has long been at war against workers, as it seeks to drive down labor income. The offshoring of jobs, once-rare massive layoffs now routine, companies fighting unions (which we speak of in passive voice, as unions mysteriously "declining"), full-time jobs turned into part-time and contingent work, and the looming force of automation—all these tend to be reported on as unrelated, like cold fronts moving in, rather than as the many skirmishes of a long war.

Automating jobs out of existence is a new Manifest Destiny, a process discussed as though it's somehow inevitable, its victims quietly invisible in the unstoppable march of progress.

Rendering the Real World Invisible

If capital bias presses down upon workers, its pressure on the natural world is more implacable, and more hidden. Financial statements—and the stock market value based on those statements—render the natural world invisible. When the stock market falls 20 or 30 percent, headlines blare the news. The number of insects worldwide has fallen an estimated 75 percent over fifty years, and this went unnoticed for decades. Stock prices are instantly available, across countless portals. Imprecise insect counts are available only occasionally, from obscure groups like Germany's Krefeld Society of Entomologists.[13]

Stock prices reflect reality for the wealthiest 10 percent who possess 89 percent of holdings.[14] Insect counts represent the reality of ecosystems on which all life depends. As EO Wilson put it, without insects the environment would collapse into chaos, resulting in starvation on an unimaginable scale.[15]

Insects are not assets of DuPont; industrial chemicals are. Since DuPont is part of the S&P 500, and since S&P index funds are held in many 401(k) plans and institutional portfolios, we're implicitly hoping the value of chemical assets will increase as we hope for these portfolios to rise. The insect apocalypse is designed in.[16]

Also designed in is the way climate change action is blocked by oil companies. The protection of investor and corporate "rights" includes the rights of oil firms. After Italy banned new coastal oil drilling, the UK oil company Rockhopper sued the Italian government for the loss of "future anticipated profits." The government was forced to pay the firm £210 million—thirty-three times the amount the firm invested in the blocked project.[17]

The Danger of Not Naming

If naming can trap us, it can also help to free us. Indeed, there's an insidious danger in *not* naming. Without challenging the bias woven through the system, our change efforts may at best be inadequate. At worst, they may legitimize the system as it is, delaying transformation.

I say this after more than thirty years as a journalist, theorist, and consultant advocating progressive business and responsible investing. I've observed up close how the system has forced those of us working for change to keep our discourse inside the paradigm-as-is.

Environmental consultants to corporations are reluctant to say ecosystems matter because life matters. They emphasize to corporations how sustainability practices impact risk, cost savings, and brand positioning and thus *can improve the bottom line.* Corporate social responsibility (CSR) leaders and ethics officers speak of how good practices protect reputation and *enhance profits.*

Even among impact investors—the most radical among ethical investors, committed to making deliberate, positive impact with their investments—two-thirds say they seek *"market rate" returns.* Implicitly, what they/we are saying (what investment advisors may intimidate us into believing) is that profits must never suffer.[18] Even if such profits are the force advancing ecological crisis and worker suffering.

I've been part of these various corporate whisperer communities for decades. I cofounded *Business Ethics* magazine in 1987 because I believed good businesspeople could change the world, and I met many trying to do so. As I interviewed company founders and leaders in corporate social responsibility, sustainability, ethics, and responsible investing, I heard often about the struggle to make the business case—to speak the lingua franca of the system, trying to convince it to change. I penned a 2004 piece titled, "Holy Grail Found: Absolute, Definitive Proof CSR Pays Off." Reviewing findings from two massive metastudies, I wrote that "thirty years and 112 studies later," it had been proven: CSR goes hand in hand with financial outperformance.[19]

That was nearly two decades ago, but the question is still being asked: Will responsible investing result in lower returns? Our answers make no difference. The *question itself* keeps us within the old paradigm, where gains to capital come first. We're forced to explain, beseechingly: no matter what social change we seek, financial income will never be compromised.

This enforced submission to capital bias has entrapped and enfeebled all the fields of corporate whispering, even as these fields have flourished as career paths. I've known these fields since their infancy. I went to a meeting of the Social Investing Forum in 1989, at that time the field's only trade association, when the sum total of attendees was sixteen, all of us fitting around one conference table. SRI is today called ESG (encompassing environmental, social, and governance issues), and the field boasts $35 trillion in assets—a third of global assets under management, loosely defined.[20] You could attend a conference every month, if you were foolish enough to want to.

Over my years at *Business Ethics* and my more recent years at the Democracy Collaborative, I have watched fields like corporate social responsibility and sustainability consulting similarly grow into massive professional communities. I saw most major corporations add ethics officers. I watched as CSR and sustainability reporting templates were designed from scratch, and by 2019, 90 percent of corporations in the S&P 500 published such reports.[21]

Over the same years, I saw corporations to which I'd given Business Ethics Awards hire union-busting attorneys, send jobs overseas, do massive layoffs once considered anathema, send executive pay into the stratosphere. Demand tax cuts from cities simply to stay, or in order to move. Lobby against the very values—like environmental sustainability—companies professed to embrace. All the while plastics were filling the ocean, birds were disappearing, coral reefs were dying, and carbon emissions were soaring. And worker income was stagnating.

Resistance Is Futile

All of these change efforts are admirable. These are good people doing good work. Yet that work has failed to touch the essence of the system. The reverse happened: the system subsumed change efforts into itself. The metaphor that springs to mind is from old *Star Trek* episodes featuring the Borg, the spacefaring race of cybernetic organisms who traveled the galaxies in massive, metallic, cube-shaped spaceships; as they encountered other species and worlds, they absorbed everything into the Borg collective. All creatures, all worlds, were to become part of this single giant machine. The Borg's motto: "resistance is futile."

The Borg most recently has captured nearly the entire field of responsible investing. This field was created by people like the fierce and visionary founder of Trillium Asset Management and other key organizations in the field, the late Joan Bavaria, with whom my wife worked for seventeen years; we socialized regularly with Joan and her partner in the years before she died. Joan never failed to take a controversial stand when it was right—standing up for gay rights, for example, long before it was fashionable. She and others like her created the vision of using capital to change the world, and today's subfields of impact investing and shareholder activism retain that visionary spirit. ESG too often does not.

In a powerful exposé, "The ESG Mirage," *Bloomberg Businessweek* showed how the concept of ESG has been hollowed out. The story told of how MSCI, the largest ESG rating company, has inverted the meaning of social and ecological impact. The original idea was to measure the impact of business on society and the environment. But MSCI's ESG measures now do the opposite: they measure how social and ecological problems *will impact corporations and shareholders.*

Consider what it means when MSCI raises a company ecological rating based on "water stress." We might think this means the company is putting less stress on water systems. Wrong. It measures *whether there is sufficient water to sustain production.*[22]

Translation: clean water matters if it benefits corporations. And corporations exist to benefit capital. That's the Borg of capital bias capturing sustainability.

Of all the money retail investors have invested in sustainable or ESG funds globally, an estimated 60 percent has gone into funds using MSCI ratings. The "sustainable" companies making it into these ESG funds include nearly 90 percent of the S&P 500.[23]

I'm sorry to say I aided and abetted this swindle. With others, I spent decades trying to prove ethical investing/ESG would enhance profits, and MSCI took us at our word. ESG ratings now are *only* about enhancing profits.

Cognitive scientist George Lakoff put the problem this way: *when we invoke the frame, we reinforce the frame.*[24] When we whisper into executive and investor ears that capital income will only be enhanced, we deliver a message fatal to change: capital must come first.

Fixes That Failed

Bloomberg Businessweek's exposé is one of a growing number of challenges to fields like ESG, CSR, corporate sustainability, and philanthropy. On one side, these critiques come from the hard right, challenging ESG as illegitimate.[25] But within the field, the more interesting critiques represent the beginning of a sea change. Professionals who once embraced strategies of "win-win," "doing well by doing good," "green growth," and "shared value" are beginning to challenge these narratives.

ESG, CSR and other efforts for voluntary change are a "fix that fails," wrote Duncan Austin, who spent fourteen years at Generation Investment Management, the sustainable investment firm cofounded by Al Gore. Austin said we need to graduate quickly from these shallow responses to "deeper responses of policy and culture change."[26]

Another canary in the coal mine is Tariq Fancy, the former chief investment officer for sustainable investing at BlackRock, the world's largest asset management firm, who went public with a withering critique of ESG, calling it a "dangerous fantasy" to believe profits and progress will "magically overlap on their own."[27]

The "elite charade of changing the world" was taken on by Anand Giridharadas in his best-selling book *Winners Take All*. He wrote of how "idea festivals sponsored by plutocrats and big business" promote "private and voluntary half-measures," an approach that "not only fails to make things better, but also serves to keep things as they are."[28]

New York Times writer Peter Goodman wrote about how "Davos Man" billionaires pulled off one of the greatest heists in history, enriching themselves as they piously spouted platitudes at the World Economic Forum about their devotion to serving all "stakeholders."

Philanthropist Edgar Villanueva's book *Decolonizing Wealth* created a sensation in his field as he wrote scathingly that philanthropy "is (we are) a sleepwalking sector, white zombies spewing the money of dead white people." With grant decisions made solely by powerful elites, he called philanthropy "colonialism in the empire's newest clothes," which, despite its altruistic façade, "actually further divides and destabilizes society."[29]

Ralph Thurm—formerly a sustainability executive at Siemens and Deloitte, now heading up the nonprofit platform r3.0—has written of "ESG Lalaland" and how it may do "irrevocable damage to sustainability." His critique was saluted by many in the field, even as he termed the current economic system "a slow suicide pact."[30]

Six business school and public policy professors similarly issued an ominous warning:

> [The] massive growth of corporate sustainability programs under the business case is not benign. It is a cancer. The longer it metastasizes and continues to crowd out healthier interventions, the greater the risk that it will kill our prospect of pulling back from environmental disaster.[31]

Social Democracy Is Being Blown Away

If change whispering from within is proving a chimera, managing capitalism from without is faltering as well. Social democracy in Europe—long celebrated as the needed alternative to US capitalism—is today experiencing "system-wide blight," wrote journalist and Brandeis professor Robert Kuttner in *The American Prospect*, the publication he cofounded.[32]

In the postwar years, social democracy was a largely successful effort to create livable societies. Yet as a system, it never took on the task of transforming the ownership and DNA of corporations and capital markets. In its original vision, socialism emphasized control of the means of production. But throughout Europe this was gradually watered down into "managed" capitalism. Important islands of public ownership were created, like the UK's National Health Service

(NHS). Strong welfare systems were built in many countries, particularly France. Powerful unions represented more than half of workers in places like Belgium and the Nordic countries of Sweden, Finland, Denmark, and Norway. Workers won board seats and representation on works councils in Austria and Germany.

All these remain important countervailing forces to capitalism. But it's time to go beyond them. In all these countries, private companies and capital markets were left largely in place, their internal focus on maximizing gains for capital left mostly unchanged. As that relentless machine of capital extraction expanded globally, the pressure reached into social democracy.

Capitalism made the lives of ordinary people more precarious, leaving struggling citizens with fewer reasons to vote for social democrats. At the same time, the hard right waged a long and in some ways successful war on social democracy. In Finland, trade union density fell from 80 percent to 59 percent. In the UK, there are efforts to defund and privatize the NHS. In France, there's pressure to weaken the pension system. Even socialist and labor parties in Europe have in many ways drifted from their commitment to social democracy.[33]

By 2021, the social democratic vote across most of continental Europe had shrunk to 20 percent or less. The French Socialist Party, the German SPD, the Labour Party in the UK—all saw a hemorrhaging of the support they once enjoyed. Even those nations closer to actual socialism, such as Sweden, are in trouble. As Swedish author Elisabeth Asbrink wrote, election gains by the hard right signal "the end of Swedish exceptionalism."[34]

In Europe "the democratic left is all but dead," Kuttner concluded. The old order of social democracy is in the process of collapsing. Its destroyer is capitalism.[35]

Solutions Fail to Cohere

Meanwhile, capitalism itself is increasingly unstable and deeply in trouble—a fact widely acknowledged, at the highest levels. In her Day

One message to staff in 2021, President Biden's Treasury Secretary Janet Yellen spoke of "four historic crises" facing the US: the pandemic, the climate crisis, systemic racism, and "an economic crisis that has been building for 50 years."[36]

Ingenious technical policy solutions abound. But if such policies are to gain political traction, they require a movement built on a deep understanding of capitalism as a system. We don't yet have that. Even at its apex in the New Deal, the American liberal tradition lacked this deep, systemic understanding.[37]

Today there's a common tendency to blame individual billionaires, individual companies, bad actors who break the rules. Or, as progressives, to focus on 1930s-style interventions like taxation, minimum wages, unions, regulation, and antitrust, which largely leave the DNA of the extractive system intact.

The core of the modern economy is corporations and capital markets. That's the essence of the financialized property regime sapping society's resilience. How do we rebuild that core property regime to serve the common good, so it still functions in economic terms? That's a challenge we've yet to fully take on, even to fully envision. How do we shift to broad-based forms of democratic ownership, enabling us to own our future? How do we shift the role of capital so it's no longer in charge but in service to the public good?

Those seeking change have yet to coherently, collectively dream of a next system. We're not dreaming at the scale of the problem. We've been thinking small—trying to get along with capitalism, to make it a bit less bad. We've been working for voluntary change at the portfolio level. Or focusing on individual companies. Mostly working for incremental change, sector by sector, issue by issue, rather than imagining together a next system and advancing toward it along workable pathways.

As George Monbiot put it in the *Guardian*, it's not that system change is too big an ask, or that it takes too long. "The problem is that incrementalism is too small an ask." It's too small to drive deep change. Too small to stop the tidal wave of revolutionary change from the hard right. Too small to break the delusions and silences that entrap us.[38]

Moral Capitalism Is as Impossible as Moral Racism

Instead of system change, many are calling today for what amounts to a gentler version of the system-as-is. Liberal economist Branko Milanovic, who researched income inequality for the World Bank for nearly two decades and now teaches at City University of New York, writes that all economic systems today are capitalist, that even communism was a way-station to capitalism, and that all we can hope for is to soften it around the edges so it evolves into a "people's capitalism" or an "egalitarian capitalism."

President Biden, unveiling a plan to raise taxes on corporations and billionaires, reassured the nation, "I'm a capitalist."[39] Pope Francis is working with multimillionaire Lynn Forester de Rothschild, encouraging business leaders to adopt *inclusive capitalism*. Michael Kazin, formerly editor of the leftist *Dissent* magazine, in his latest book terms his egalitarian vision "moral capitalism."[40]

There's a reason we don't talk about "moral racism" or "egalitarian sexism" or "rethinking imperialism." We know these are impossible. A system of bias cannot be made moral.

Capitalism is a system of bias. Bias isn't a minor feature or a side effect but the system's deep nature. The implication is clear: moral capitalism is impossible. What we need isn't improved capitalism but a next system.

4

CALLING OUT THE
DEEP FORCES AT WORK

*White Supremacy Entangled
with Wealth Supremacy*

DURING THE EARLY DAYS of the Biden administration, amid the rollout of an initial $1.9 trillion COVID pandemic stimulus package, controversy sprang up around a planned $4 billion in debt relief for farmers of color. The press reported that white farmers had sued the USDA, alleging reverse racial discrimination. Soon the debt forgiveness was tied up in the courts, where it remains, dragging the farmers closer to losing their land.[1]

This wasn't the whole story.

As I dug deeper, I found those "white farmers" were being used by conservative groups like the shady America First Foundation, founded by former Trump aides. Its explicit purpose was suing the Biden administration. The group's website had the feel of a fake front group, all about "taking America back"—yes, taking it from disadvantaged farmers, and keeping it for the Gatsbyesque wealth of Trump, his dark money donors, and the corporate beneficiaries of his tax cuts and deregulation.[2]

Still, this wasn't the whole story.

There was another layer, deeper. Quieter. Something I glimpsed in passing—something that likely seemed a side story to most.

A second objection to the "injustice" of the debt forgiveness came from bankers. It wasn't racism (or it wasn't *only* racism) that made these bankers pout. They claimed that having loans paid off early—paid in full, including all interest due—would deprive the banks and their investors of the stream of income they'd planned on.[3]

Not only were the banks to receive large chunks of ready cash, which they could relend at interest—leaving their business model intact—but the government planned the extraordinary step of paying them *120 percent* of the amounts due. They'd get the principal they'd loaned, all interest owed, *plus* 20 percent to compensate for taxes and fees and bother.

Where, we might ask, is the difficulty in this scenario? Still, in the bankers' minds—in their understanding of their financial "rights"—the future income to be extracted from the backs of struggling Black farmers was sacrosanct. They argued its "loss" should be compensated.

This was wealth supremacy. Bias toward protection of capital. This basic system inclination is easy to miss, because it's subtle—deeper than the shenanigans of today's hard right, though circuitously related to it. It's the sense of entitlement among the guardians of wealth that rarely shows its face, a form of privilege so confident and accepted that it has no need to declare itself. As hard as it is to see, deep capital bias is one of the most profound forces at work in this story.

Tracking the Real Losses

We might ask: Why didn't the bankers find satisfaction in the fact that their clients' borrowing needs would be fulfilled? Indeed, had the lending institutions been owned by their depositors, as credit unions are; or owned by the state, as is the Bank of North Dakota; or been chartered to serve the disadvantaged, as are community development financial institutions (CDFIs), then, yes, serving client needs would be their purpose. But investor-owned banks, by and large, are designed to serve investor "needs." Which means extracting as much as possible from clients.

Thus, the bankers were aggrieved that their extraction had been disrupted, as a tick removed from a dog might complain its meal had been cut short.

The truth is, the banks faced no real losses. The same can't be said of the Black farmers. The few who had debts—which is to say, the few who'd hung onto their land—were a vanishing remnant of a ghost legion already wiped out.

Since 1920, the number of Black-owned farms has dropped from roughly a million to fewer than forty thousand. Those losses can be traced to causes like corporate takeover of the agriculture industry in a wave of consolidation, and the burdensome loan terms and high foreclosure rates by lenders. In these processes, investor-owned Big Ag firms and investor-owned lenders gained. Black farming families lost their land. While banks played a role, so too did the Department of Agriculture, which Black farmers termed the nation's "last plantation."[4]

What the missing nine hundred thousand Black farming families experienced was real loss: loss of family land, loss of a way of life, loss of a place in the sun to call their own, loss of subsistence income that would have sustained these families through their sweat and toil. *That* loss—total loss—was of little concern to the bankers. It didn't appear on the radar screen of their Bloomberg terminals. Their concern was loss of *capital income*.

When Black-owned farmland had been seized through the antiseptically brutal processes of bankruptcy and foreclosure, bankers viewed it as unfortunate necessity. Yet the most minuscule disruption to capital income—which the bankers believed must be smooth, predictable, reliable—now, *that* was unacceptable. These "hard" financial processes were not to be disturbed by "soft" human issues, like the Department of Agriculture trying to alleviate suffering its practices had caused, suffering to which the banks themselves had contributed.

We see here how capital income dwells in a universe apart, bearing no trace of the hardship it leaves in its wake.

Learning to See in Systems

Naming and seeing the extractive system at work in this scenario means pausing a moment, paying attention to that glimpse out of the corner of the eye. It means lingering over the instinctive bias of the bankers, seeing past the individuals into the architecture of the system itself—recognizing that system at work, how its investor-centric design naturally gave rise to the bankers' complaints and to the perils Black and brown farmers face.

In the background of this story are other institutions of the extractive system: the investor-owned Big Ag corporations, which see their purpose as creating maximum income for investors. These corporations have been out there a long time, consolidating the industry, raising prices for seed and fertilizer, and paying as little as possible for the grain or corn from farmers, in many ways squeezing out those Black farmers.

In this story of loan forgiveness, it looks initially like white farmers are thwarting the process. But when we name the deeper system forces at work, we understand that Black and white farmers have both been losing a long time, while investor-owned corporations and investor-owned banks have been winning. The invisible players here are investors. They don't have to lift a finger, because the system is always working quietly on their behalf.

Where is the democratic economy in this story? One place is debt relief, which is a critical pathway of democratizing finance (explored more in chapter 16). It's an important form of assistance—but it's also short term. It's after the fact. It doesn't touch the core of the system.

The long-term solution is structural. It's about the design of those corporations and banks working against the farmers. To envision this deep, structural, system-level solution takes an act of imagination. It means picturing, for example, lending institutions that could have been operating here and weren't. Or more firms like the $1 billion Organic Valley, a dairy marketing cooperative owned by 1,800 organic family farms, working for rather than against farmers.

In a democratic economy, bankers would be working to *keep* Black farmers on the land. In Mondragon—the massive worker-owned cooperative system in Spain, with several hundred companies and nearly eighty thousand employees—the cooperative bank *lowers* interest rates when a worker-owned business is in trouble. Borrower-centered financing works. In the US, CDFIs do it all the time. Lending need not be the form of violence it often is.

Integrating into a Burning House

There's something else here it's important to name. System change likely isn't our real goal in this situation. It's not the thing that gets us out of bed in the morning. But system change is the vehicle that ultimately protects and advances what we really care about, like racial equity.

There's an analogy to climate change. When a hurricane hits, our first response is to get people off rooftops, bring them blankets, find them housing. But if that's all we do, we're condemning these people to more and bigger hurricanes to come. Similarly, debt forgiveness for Black farmers brings immediate relief. But if that's all we offer, we're condemning them to larger struggles to come as the ongoing, relentless extraction of wealth by Big Ag and big banks continues.

When our goal is to remedy racial injustice, we can't effectively aid these farmers by solving only for racial bias while leaving capital bias intact.

Martin Luther King Jr. came to this realization as, late in his life, he began planning his Poor People's Campaign, widening his concern to embrace economic injustice for all the dispossessed. In a dialogue with Harry Belafonte, he expressed confidence about winning the battle for integration. But without transforming the broader economic system, he said he feared "I am integrating my people into a burning house."[5]

It's important to see and name how white supremacy is entangled with wealth supremacy. The bankers in the loan forgiveness story may well have been racially biased; they may have been quicker to foreclose on Black farmers than whites. But that's only one bias at work here. When the bankers instinctively and structurally favor the interests of investors, they're working against people of color and all those without substantial property. Racial bias is entwined with capital bias.

Property as a Distinct System of Discrimination

For centuries, these two biases, hand in hand, have served to dispossess people of color through the merciless histories of colonialism, the slave trade, plantations, the taking of Indigenous land, predatory lending, gentrification, and more. If many of us now understand the racism threaded through these processes, it's when we adjust our eyes a bit that we see how these acts of racism were deployed along with a second, complementary force: the cultural construct of *property*—who is permitted or forbidden to own property, who is turned into property, who is deprived of property without recourse, who is denied the vote because they don't own property, who finds that the fruits of their own labor is legally the property of another.

Systems of property and systems of race feed upon each other. Yet property and race systems are also distinct—overlapping while operating separately, functioning by different logic.

It's important to grasp this different logic. White supremacy *persists*, inflicting harm across generations. Wealth supremacy *accelerates*. Because the larger the sphere of swollen wealth becomes, the greater extraction it requires in order to grow larger still. If people of color have long been and remain primary targets for this extraction, today our society and the planet itself are caught in its iron grip.

The suffering that people of color have long known is hitting white people. White farmers are also now losing land. In Wisconsin, where largely white-owned dairy farms were once among the nation's most prosperous, the last decade saw an alarming 40 percent of dairy farms go under.[6] As the Institute for Local Self-Reliance documented, at the root are concentrated corporate power and lending practices, the same forces that worked against Black farmers.[7] As investors gain, family farms lose.

As the story of debt forgiveness continued, Biden's original plan never did pass Congress. Yet later, Biden managed to enact legislation that accomplished much of the same goal. Compared to the original package, it provided more funding overall for loan adjustments, but less to remedy past discrimination—with debt relief based solely on need, not race. The upshot was less ideal for the Black farmers, and a class action lawsuit was filed. But hopefully the relief gave many a chance to hold onto their land.[8]

There are large lessons here.

Naming the deep system at work in this scenario, we can see how the lending needs of all small business, not just farmers, are ill-served by the infrastructure of the extractive economy. The US once had a thriving network of locally owned banks, rooted in community—18,000 in 1985. By the end of 2020, the tally dwindled to fewer than 4,400. These banks were harvested, mashed up into the big Wall Street banks that dominate today, like JPMorgan Chase, Bank of America, and Citigroup. These big banks are supported by our deposits. It's our money, our communities' money, that makes up their assets. Yet because mammoth absentee banks are less connected to community, they're less likely to extend loans to small local businesses, which today struggle for access to capital.[9] Combating racism in itself will not solve this system problem.

The final piece is about recognizing ourselves in the operation of the current system.

The year the bankers protested Black farmer debt relief, investors did extremely well. If we hold index funds, those investors included us. The S&P Bank Index rose a jaw-dropping 34 percent, and the

S&P 500 overall was up 27 percent that year.[10] Those of us with some retirement savings no doubt cheered the good news. When the market soon plunged into bear territory, we held our breath and hoped for the good times to return. What else were we to dream of?

PART II

THE MYTHS OF WEALTH SUPREMACY

WHEN WE STOP SHORT of seeing and naming wealth supremacy, we risk inadvertently supporting it. We leave capital to function on autopilot, like a runaway train.

For such a system to work its destructive ways, no actual malice is required. Yes, there are many—CEOs, financiers, billionaires—who work to block change and profit exorbitantly from the system as it is. Such people need to be held to account. Yet bias is larger than any set of individuals. The system of wealth supremacy is propelled by tremendous inertia—hurtling down a track with the engineer mostly asleep at the controls.

The track the train runs on is mindset. Narrative. Culture. Those things "everyone knows" to be true.

Those working for change often point to the greed of CEOs, corporations, and billionaires. Individual greed is real. Yet the larger issue is how the system normalizes and institutionalizes greed. The practices of financialized capitalism operate inside a seemingly benign narrative of technocratic mathematics, which lends greed authority and persistence. Rendering its casual brutality invisible.

When you're piloting an institutional portfolio—much as someone pilots a mechanized bomber at fifty thousand feet— you're not sowing destruction, you're pressing buttons and hitting targets; you're not destroying jobs and small businesses, you're moving assets up the risk-return spectrum to achieve target returns.

Narratives provide order. They can also carry invisible malignancy—as in the narrative of "whiteness" we live invisibly within. Whiteness is an institutionalized system of power, says Robin DiAngelo. It's integral to a worldview that normalizes the domination of whites over people of color. The pervasiveness of this bias tends to elude notice for white people, she observed, because it's carried through cultural practices that tend to be unmarked and unnamed.[1]

Wealth supremacy tends also to be unmarked and unnamed, dwelling so deep in our culture as to be imperceptible. History helps us to see such things. As T. S. Eliot said, history gives us a "perception not only of the pastness of the past, but of its presence."[2]

Wealth supremacy and capital bias did not spring sui generis into our culture with the advent of tech billionaires, nor even with the dawn of the Industrial Revolution. This bias carries the mindset of centuries past that infused the world of Great Britain and America into which capitalism was birthed—the world where Black bodies were treated as property; where women were not citizens and largely forbidden to own property; where the white, male, propertied elite in England's Parliament made themselves the preeminent power in 1688 as they unseated one king and chose another. It's no accident that the founders of capitalism are described as robber "barons" and "kings" of capital. The aim of these wealthy men was not to subvert the privileges of the landed class but to replicate those privileges for themselves.

The worldview of the British propertied elite was one where British theorist Edmund Burke—the philosophical father of conservatism—scorned the "seditious" doctrine of democracy, that "delusive, gypsey" right of the people to govern themselves. The nation's property owners represented the "settled, permanent substance" of the nation, Burke asserted; hence, the wealthy were the rightful rulers. If the "swinish multitude"— the hairdresser, the candlemaker—were permitted to rule, it would "pervert the natural order of things."[3]

The very idea of democracy, Burke feared, could have "the pernicious consequence of destroying all docility" in those unsuited for citizenship. The lower orders were to be kept in their places. And those lower orders, as historian Don Herzog noted, explicitly included women, Black people, Jewish people, and workers.[4]

As the social compact of Burke's day was narrated by the landed class, the world of business and investing in our day is narrated by the capitalist class—by the owners and managers of wealth. It's a world built on the logic of a particular set of concepts, which tend to be seen as the natural order of things, something akin to the law of gravity.

To master the language and mindset of these concepts is to enter the symbolic order of finance and business; to question these notions is to risk being branded an unsophisticated outsider.

These concepts are wrapped in myths—the deep myths of our property regime. When we unmask them, we see how each invisibly encodes capital bias, and how the soul of these myths is rooted in the predemocratic world of aristocracy and empire.

The Myths of Wealth Supremacy

The Myth of Maximizing   No amount of financial wealth is ever enough. We call this "return on investment." It is ideally maximum, limitless, and perpetual.

The Myth of Fiduciary Duty   The most sacred duty is that owed by the managers of wealth to the owners of wealth, the "fiduciary duty" to protect and expand capital, no matter the consequences to society or the planet.

The Myth of Corporate Governance   Workers are not members of the corporation. In corporate governance, membership is reserved for capital owners, while workers are disenfranchised and dispossessed.

The Myth of the Income Statement   Income to capital ("profit") is always to be increased, while income to labor ("expense") is always to be decreased. These are implicit rules of the income statement.

The Myth of Materiality   Gains to capital are real ("material"), while social and ecological damages are not real (not material) except to the extent they affect capital. This is among the rules of corporate and financial accounting.

The Myth of the Free Market   Democracy is to be subdued, for it is the enemy of the independence and power of wealth. There shall be no limits on the field of action of corporations and capital. We call this a "free market."

The Myth of Takings   The first duty of government is the protection of wealth. The US Constitution prohibits "takings" from the propertied elite, while that elite may take from others at will.

5

NO AMOUNT OF WEALTH IS EVER ENOUGH

The Myth of Maximizing

Remembering Descartes, I set out to
doubt everything I had been taught.

—MARION MILNER

"IN DREAMS BEGIN RESPONSIBILITIES," wrote W. B. Yeats. If Europe once dreamed of colonization as a benevolent civilizing force, today we dream of ever-expanding "wealth creation" as similarly benign—portfolios swelling forever, rational, clean, wondrous.

Suffused throughout the culture, such a dream creates a veneer of truth. It seems possible that such a magical machine might exist—and look, there it is: MacKenzie Scott, ex-wife of Amazon founder Jeff Bezos, giving away $8.5 billion in less than a year and ending up with more wealth than she began with.[1] What could be wrong with such abundance? In it we hear murmurs of something soothing about our world. Magic is real, if only we too could touch its hem.

In business and investing—the world where the dream of wealth creation is operationalized—the myth takes on a harder edge. It is expressed as a core *purpose*, a central system design rule that must be followed. It's taught in business schools as a kind of commandment: the goal of business management is *maximizing returns to shareholders*. In investing, the myth is often expressed as *creating maximum risk-adjusted returns*, the assumed purpose of portfolio management.

This is the myth of maximizing.

THE MYTH OF MAXIMIZING

No amount of financial wealth is ever enough. We call this "return on investment." It is ideally maximum, limitless, and perpetual.

This myth embodies the core system design element of *reverence for wealth*. We see the mythic quality of this belief in the way our culture rarely looks upon wealth accumulation as we might look upon, say, gluttons gorging on food. No, rich people insatiably ingesting financial income is good. Perhaps the ultimate good.

This myth is reinforced by asset owners like foundations, pension funds, and university endowments, as well as asset managers like the giant BlackRock, and us ourselves, as they and we look at investment statements and shift assets away from those "performing poorly," or abandon mutual funds and investment advisors that "underperform" benchmarks.

Maximizing is the norm around which the entire system is organized. The myth of its beneficence, its necessity, is in the air, capturing and infusing our thinking. When maximizing is going well, when we're on its winning side, it can induce a kind of delirium, like alcoholic bliss, so intoxicating as to put us in a state of amnesia about the real world, other people, all that actually matters.

We know the face of maximizing best in the guise of billionaires, a phenomenon not limited to the US, Britain, Japan, and other classically capitalist nations. It's virtually worldwide. Russia's invasion of Ukraine was spawned by a billionaire, Vladimir Putin, entwined with billionaire oligarchs. Nominally communist China has more than one hundred billionaires in its top advisory group and legislature.[2] Beijing has more billionaires than any city in the world.[3] Donald Trump played a billionaire on TV. The Koch network of dark money is about billionaires marshalling the wealth of other billionaires. It may not be an overstatement to say billionaires rule the world.

Elon Musk—at one point the world's richest person—in a single year of the COVID pandemic gained some $118 billion. Mind you, that was what he *gained*, not his total wealth. In the same year, the United Nations estimated that 150 million people fell into poverty.[4]

Still, the insidiousness of maximizing lies not simply in its pursuit by those we comfortably regard as villains. The danger is in how maximizing is embedded at the core of a global system—and in the myths we unwittingly embrace in our own hearts that validate that system.

Gigantism and Elephantiasis

Looking into these three words—*maximum, limitless, perpetual*—we see how the principle of maximizing mimics the worldview of imperialism.

To extract *maximum* amount from each possession, each colony, each asset, means taking from wherever and whomever you can to benefit the self, and to benefit others in the small elite holding substantial wealth. In the East India Company, this principle was in force as the company looted the entire treasury of Bengal, sending it down the Ganges in one hundred boats, in a financial coup that doubled the company's share price on the London Stock Exchange overnight. That was one act in the fifty-year process by which a for-profit corporation—"an empire within an empire," as one of its directors put it—enriched shareholders by reducing India to a British possession, extracting from it every conceivable ounce of wealth.[5]

Milking each asset to the extreme: that's the first part of maximizing. Then, the quantity and kind of assets also need to *limitlessly* expand. The capture of the entire globe was the aim of European empire. Under the explosive power of the Industrial Revolution, with its relentless seeking of raw materials and new markets, European colonial powers entered their final convulsive spasm of "New Imperialism" growth—until by 1914, they controlled 85 percent of the globe as colonies and possessions. This expansionist surge included the bloody scramble for Africa, as Europeans captured virtually that entire continent within three to four decades, crushing Indigenous cultures with consequences that endure to this day.[6] In this globalizing impulse we see the deeply entwined nature of what Guyanese intellectual Walter Rodney termed the "capitalist/imperialist system."[7]

Today, finance capital seeks similarly to limitlessly extend itself. Historian James Belich referred to this ethos as the Anglo propensity to "gigantism" and "elephantiasis."[8]

Cecil Rhodes, a master of empire as well as a capitalist entrepreneur, exemplified this spirit as he led his private army on military expeditions, almost singlehandedly expanding the British empire by 450,000 square miles, an area larger than Texas and California combined. He also personally claimed dominion over the mineral riches of Africa, acquiring diamond mines on land forcibly taken by the British from African peoples. In the process, Rhodes accumulated one of the greatest fortunes in the world, becoming chairman of the De Beers diamond company, which into the early twenty-first century exercised monopoly control over the global diamond trade. Today, De Beers operates in thirty-five countries, with 2022 revenues of $6.6 billion, still based in substantial part on extracting from former British colonies such as Botswana, Namibia, and South Africa.[9]

For Rhodes, even the planet itself was too small. He told a journalist of his sadness that nearly all the globe had been colonized. Foreshadowing the era when billionaires Richard Branson, Jeff Bezos, and Elon Musk would seek to rocket themselves into space, Rhodes pointed to the stars and said, "I would annex the planets if I could."[10]

So, as assets are milked to the extreme and as their reach expands without limit, even to the stars, then the system adds a third element: these processes ideally continue without cease, *perpetually*. We see this in our cultural myth that portfolios of assets grow beyond the death of their owner, generation upon generation, into some hoped-for infinity.

Thus the right of capital extraction is understood to be, like the divine right of kings, eternal.

Maximizing R Us

If billionaires are the masters of maximizing, the myth of maximizing—telling us how normal it is—is far more widely embraced. Maximizing is the game played by CEOs who once rolled in the clover of compensation 20 times average worker pay, then pushed for more until it reached the ludicrous heights of 350 times worker pay.[11]

Maximizing is the game of landlords raising rents 30 percent amid the COVID pandemic.[12] Maximizing is the college enjoying endowment gains of 65 percent one year, while its board didn't appear to ask: Where did all this come from, and what havoc was wreaked to obtain it?[13]

Maximizing is the S&P 500—the largest, most iconic companies in the US—bringing in aggregate investor gains of a jaw-dropping 29 percent in 2021, while these companies' asset value was growing because they were swallowing other businesses, buying out competitors, locking in near-monopoly power in sector after sector. Meanwhile, we were busy sliding our investments into index funds, hoping to see those innocent numbers rise without cease.[14]

Maximizing is the collective madness that drives the repetitive creation of stock market bubbles, which always burst—each crash bigger than the last—even as we keep revving the machine back up. We're in need of that fix.

So, yes, maximizing is widely practiced, but the fact that it's widely *accepted* is what marks it as a cultural bias. At work is the finance-colored lens that defines normality, lulling us into accepting the unacceptable. As the investment portfolios of billionaires rise, say, 7 percent—bringing $70 million in new wealth for each billion—our tiny portfolios of, say, $100,000, rise an "equal" amount of 7 percent, bringing us $7,000.

Thus we delight at the crumbs we get, while the wealthy gorge themselves at the banquet table.

There is a kind of blindness to others at the heart of maximizing. In Rhodes's day, this took the form of a virulent, institutionalized racism. When Rhodes became prime minister of the Cape Colony in southern Africa, he believed Indigenous Africans in the colony should be governed, as he wrote, as "a subject race."[15] For Rhodes's role in governing the Cape Colony, South African writer Stan Winer, echoing other critics, dubbed him "the architect of apartheid fascism."[16]

If inferior races were a myth at the heart of the imperialist worldview, at the heart of our capital-centric worldview today stands the myth of the isolated self, which tells us we exist apart from the community that nourishes us, separate from the natural world that makes our life possible. The image is of a self with a bottomless need for aggrandizement, protection, comfort. In the grip of such obsession—what Buddhists call the spirit of a "hungry ghost" that can never be satisfied—the "other" becomes an object, the purpose of which is to enrich the grasping self.

The natural world itself, in this view, becomes an object to be mastered. As historian Duncan Bell has observed, this view of nature by imperialists was intimately entwined with racism; they believed that their demonstrated power over the natural world endowed the Anglo-Saxon people with a moral mission to govern the "inferior" races, who were "incapable of generating such Promethean feats."[17]

In the gaze of this self-aggrandizing mind, this ravenously hungry heart, reality recedes. And such blindness is now institutionalized in the capital-centric system of our time. What we are not shown, as we look at our investment statements, are the Amazon warehouses teeming with workers denied sufficient bathroom breaks, mom-and-pop businesses driven under, animals held all their lives in the cruel confinement of Big Ag farms, ocean ecosystems laid waste by oil drilling. Such reality does not appear to us in the bloodless math of portfolio gains.

Profit Making vs. Profit Maximizing

Organizing economic activity this way isn't necessary, any more than sexism is a necessary way of being a man.

A useful distinction is that between companies that are *profit making* and those that are *profit maximizing*. The need for a business to make a profit is real, as I came to appreciate in the years I ran *Business Ethics*. I incorporated that company as a C corporation, not a nonprofit, because I wanted to experience the pressures all businesspeople feel. I started out wanting to run the coolest company, bringing toys to staff meetings—tiny racecars with sticky wheels that raced down the wall. It quickly dawned on me that unless we had more money coming in than going out, we wouldn't have a business at all. My cofounder, Miriam Kniaz, and I called this our "conversion experience." We became devoted to revenue.

Still, we never believed anything goes. Our associate publisher, Jean Madson, who brought in two-thirds of our revenue via advertising and corporate sponsorships, had gotten her senior prom canceled in order to organize a Vietnam War protest. She insisted we not sell sponsorships to weapons makers, and that became our policy. Since some of those firms would have loved to run ads in an ethics magazine, we may have left an annual six figures' worth of revenue on the table—revenue we desperately needed. But we had limits.

We only did what many good businesspeople do, and what my dad had done. My father ran a small business as a supplier to the printing trade. When a long-term employee—the father of a young man I went to grade school with—became fatally ill, Dad kept him on the payroll long after the man stopped working. I remember how my father agonized when he couldn't afford to do so any longer.

Over two decades as a journalist at *Business Ethics*, I witnessed something starkly different: the less-than-human, extractive process that kicks in as companies pass beyond control by the human heart, when they shift from profit making to profit maximizing. It's like the difference between social drinking and being an alcoholic, or between politely eating a plate of hors d'oeuvre versus absconding with the entire platter.

The relentless process of maximizing tends to kick in when capital comes into control. Numbers step into the driver's seat and harms recede. (What great hors d'oeuvres you brought home, honey!) Maximizing revs up when firms go public (as shares begin trading on public stock markets), and when firms are sold to larger competitors or to private equity. In all these transactions, companies often lose their soul, becoming objects for financial extraction.

Social Mission Snuffed Out

It took me years to understand how universal this process is. How insidious. It first hit me on April 12, 2000, the day the Ben & Jerry's board felt forced by law to sell the premier socially oriented firm in America to multinational Unilever, against the wishes of cofounder and CEO Ben Cohen. In the years following, Ben & Jerry's social mission began to seep away, as Unilever laid off one in five B&J employees and stopped donating 7.5 percent of profits to the Ben & Jerry's Foundation. I'd interviewed Cohen and gone to gatherings of the Social Venture Network we both were part of, where I slept on a trundle bed in crowded staffer rooms because I couldn't afford the luxury hotels. I'd profiled him and other social entrepreneurs like Jeff Hollender of Seventh Generation, Greg Steltenpohl of Odwalla juice, and Paul Hawken of the natural gardening firm Smith & Hawken. I watched over the years as, one by one, companies like these were sucked into capital control.

Hawken—who went on to write *The Ecology of Commerce*—and his cofounder, Dave Smith, painfully witnessed how the sale of their firm to the wrong hands meant loss of social mission. Smith & Hawken was sold again and again, ending up in the hands of Scotts Miracle-Gro, after which Smith told friends to stop shopping there. When Scotts later shut the firm down, both founders expressed relief. Today the hollowed-out name of Smith & Hawken is a brand at Target.[18]

I've seen this story play out countless times. Of course, individuals and families can maximize just as ruthlessly as big capital. When Purdue Pharma pushed its deadly sales of OxyContin, it was privately held, controlled by one family, the Sacklers.

Yet when capital takes control, greed becomes nonoptional. Maximizing becomes virtually mandatory—kicking into overdrive, on autopilot. Investor demand for an endless *more* squeezes even CEOs at the largest firms. At publicly traded companies, CEOs who deliver for shareholders are made fabulously wealthy. Those who don't are fired.[19]

Feeding Businesses into the Mouth of Big Capital

Since I moved on from *Business Ethics*, I've come to see that capital snuffing out social mission is just the tip of the deeper problem. *Virtually all successful businesses end up in the maw of finance.*

There's a conveyor belt constantly functioning, which works like this: No founder lives forever. Fewer than one in three passes their business to family. Of these, only 12 percent of family firms make it to the third generation.[20] Once a founder retires or dies, most small businesses close. The rest are sold—often to competitors, some to private equity. They become morsels of extraction, often sold over and over, as Smith & Hawken was, until the original life is snuffed out. Whatever impulse for human betterment motivated the founder in that garage, profit maximizing devours that impulse.

The conveyor belt can take decades. But it feeds virtually all successful firms into the mouth of capital. Where maximizing takes over.

Sometimes a healthy, life-serving alternative prevails. Here's one story.

Coming to Our Senses

My former colleague Sarah Stranahan and I were hosting a cocktail reception in Manhattan, the night before an event we'd organized for what we called "next-generation private enterprises," companies with a living mission of serving the public good, owned broadly by workers. We'd won a research grant to study the relationship between worker ownership and ecological outcomes, and we'd stumbled upon something bigger: the potential future of enterprise design. We identified fifty-plus companies that were employee-owned benefit corporations—firms like Eileen Fisher, Clif Bar, King Arthur Flour, and Cooperative Home Care Associates—delivering demonstrably positive impact for the environment and workers.[21] These were successful companies that were living systems, designed to be beneficial to the environment and to workers. The design worked.

Fifty people, mostly top executives, came to our event, one of whom was Mandy Cabot, the founder of Dansko shoe company, a worker-owned B Corporation. I'd known Mandy since my *Business Ethics* days but had lost touch. We embraced like lost friends. When I asked what she was doing now, she said with a laugh, "I bought a rainforest."

I later reached out for an interview, finding her at home in Belize, where she and her husband, Peter, had moved during COVID. Since selling Dansko, she and Peter—Mandy in her late sixties, Peter in his seventies—were looking for impact investments. They'd often traveled to Belize and were thinking of buying a little farm in the mountains there. A broker told them one day of a rainforest on the verge of being sold to a developer. "You better sit down because it's a big one," he said.

It turned out to be 27,500 acres, bordering three preserved areas, including a jaguar preserve. The parcel Mandy and Peter were considering contained an abandoned farm with a factory for making coconut oil. They fell in love. "It's the mother of all impact investments," Mandy said with a laugh. Ten percent of the land had been previously farmed, and they began rehabilitating that farm, using permaculture and regenerative agriculture. Much of the rest they turned into the new Silk Grass Wildlife Preserve, a nonprofit that today owns 30 percent of the farm and factory, and one day will own it all. Mandy's aim is to make the farm and factory profitable enough to sustain the preserve with income in perpetuity. Belizeans—a majority of them women, at Mandy's insistence—will control the boards of the preserve and the company. The complex could one day sustain two hundred good jobs.

"We're designing it all so it's scalable," Mandy said. Not scalable as in creating maximum financial wealth, but scalable in creating living depth and breadth: leaving the soil healthier, building biodiversity, supporting pollinators, "allowing all those natural ecosystems to function at their best," she said.

One day Mandy met with Will Raap. Now deceased, he was the founder of another company, Gardener's Supply, that is also an employee-owned benefit corporation (a natural gardening firm that, unlike Smith & Hawken, has preserved its ecological mission to this day). He told Mandy: "Young lady, I have one word for you. Biochar. It really will save mankind." Biochar will take tons of biowaste from the farm (coconut shells, citrus peel, avocado pits), and through pyrolysis, turn it into briquets that will sequester carbon for thousands of years, while serving as a beneficial soil amendment.

"There's so much circularity in all this," Mandy told me. "It's like we hit the jackpot. This really is the grand finale we're so lucky to have."

There was a time Mandy had nearly sold Dansko to Timberland for $100 million, but she stepped back at the last minute. She sold later to employees, probably for somewhat less money. Much of the capital she and Peter received they're investing in Silk Grass, creating something to be held in trust for the community, for the rainforest, for the jaguars.

Mandy was born into a family with what she called "robber baron" wealth, and she spoke of how inefficient it was to pile up capital, then give some away at the end. "Wouldn't it be way more efficient" to use your business to do good, she asked. "And certainly fun, right?" Her story is a reminder that being wealthy doesn't make someone a bad person; we need not shun wealth. It's a tool for doing enormous good, particularly when used to build a system that will never again allow massive wealth to accumulate in few hands.

At Dansko, the employee-owned benefit corporation, Mandy used business to create wealth for workers and broad social benefits. Silk Grass is bigger. It's using investment, profit, trust ownership, regenerative agriculture, local governance—working together, as a system, to create flourishing, ongoing, living wealth.

In system design terms, it's a microcosm of a system built around the *purpose* of reverence for life. In terms of *ownership*, the rainforest will own itself, through a trust, with *governance* by local stewards—with profits feeding its ongoing life, not being extracted out. *Accountability* for success will mean the ongoing, thriving life of the rainforest, and the financial life of the trust itself.

Other entrepreneurs would say Mandy is leaving money on the table. "What would you say to them?" I asked her. "How much more do you need than enough? Enough is enough," she said. Mandy and Peter have left their children an inheritance. They live comfortably. And they're sinking loads into Silk Grass—including years of their lives—building something they won't own in the end. What she and Peter are interested in, she said, is "what gives you the deepest sense of joy in your life."

I saw a piece of that joy, as Mandy shared on Facebook a video of dozens of baby sea turtles, which she'd worked with others to nurture, being released to the sea.

One day, it may be that our culture looks back to find that the mania for maximizing was one of those mass delusions that lost its hold. Writing of other such delusions—the witch mania, the obsession with alchemy, the bizarre custom of duels—Charles Mackay, in *Extraordinary Popular Delusions and the Madness of Crowds*, famously observed: "Men, it is said, think in herds; it will be seen that they go mad in herds, while they only recover their senses more slowly, and one by one."

Mandy, I imagine, has indeed left loads of money on the table. Another way of putting it: she found a better use for that money.

6

EXPANDING WEALTH IS A SACRED OBLIGATION

The Myth of Fiduciary Duty

IF MAXIMIZING GAINS FOR capital is the way things are in our system—the norm around which the entire system is organized—how does this airy ideal become functional in the world? What gives clout to the dream? This brings us to a second core myth, which goes by the oddly innocent name of *fiduciary duty*.

THE MYTH OF FIDUCIARY DUTY

The most sacred duty is that owed by the managers of wealth to the owners of wealth, the "fiduciary duty" to protect and expand capital, no matter the consequences to society or the planet.

Now, admittedly, this little phrase seems boringly technical. A big so-what. But it matters hugely. In fact, it may matter more than anything else in today's ongoing, silent, relentless creation of economic injustice. Stay with me a moment as I explain why.

A fiduciary, quite simply, is someone who acts on another's behalf. When you place investments in a mutual fund or with a registered investment advisor, they have a fiduciary duty to act in your interests. The boards of pension funds are similarly investing other people's money, and are to act in the interests of those beneficiaries, not in the interests of the directors themselves. Fiduciary duties include a *duty of care* (a duty to pay attention, stay on top of materials provided, not fall asleep during board meetings) and a *duty of loyalty* (to put the client or organization's interests first and not spend their funds on a cousin's crackpot scheme or a personal vacation in the Bahamas).

Fiduciary relationships often involve the investment of assets, but not always. The attorney-client relationship is also a fiduciary one, because our lawyer is obligated to act in our interests. Directors of corporations are bound by fiduciary duties, because our system sees corporations as objects owned by shareholders. Not every investment relationship is a fiduciary one. A broker executing trades at a client's direction is not bound by fiduciary duties; that broker may try to sell you investment products *not* in your best interests so as to generate high fees to line their own pocket.

The general understanding of fiduciary duty is that it requires a trustee or investment manager to maximize gains for capital, disregarding the interests of other parties. Whether that is *actually*, legally, the requirement is subject to debate. I'll return to this later in this chapter. For now, let's just say many sophisticated legal and financial experts find the maximizing mandate to be highly questionable, or plain wrong.

But it is the myth. Many directors believe this myth, which seems to tell them: your hands are tied; your job is to protect and grow capital a maximum amount and think of nothing else.

Sorry, Hands Are Tied

It's important to unpack two different meanings tucked into the myth of fiduciary duty. One of these is actually benign. Here I mean the simple duties of care and of loyalty: the obligation to pay attention and to be prudent, not reckless, in making decisions.

These fiduciary duties are real. They are serious. And they are necessary.

But there's something else lurking here. Something nonobvious, for which fiduciary duty is a marvelous hiding place. That something else is capital bias: the idea that wealth holders matter and no one else does. That the wealthy have no obligation to anyone except themselves, and that when they hand their wealth to a fiduciary, that guardian's sole obligation is to expand the wealth without limit, to a maximum extent—never looking at who is stepped on in the process.

These days, individuals and institutions with substantial assets don't manage their own investments. This is delegated to others. Self-interest turns a corner, if you will, so it's no longer a matter of personal feelings (greed, cruelty, indifference, kindness); it's about the technical duties owed by investment managers to a mass of assets. It's about safeguarding other people's money.

Large investors—pension funds, foundation endowments, the portfolios of the wealthy managed by family offices—are seen as holding the *ownership* of the assets in question. That's a key element of system design here. When they place these assets with others, that relationship is about honoring their property rights. That brings in a second system design element of *accountability*, tied to financial impact alone.

This arrangement leaves no one feeling responsible for harms done. Not the wealthy, who need not actually grind anyone's face in the dirt; that work is done for them through multiple layers of intermediaries. Not corporate CEOs—they're simply following their ethical obligation to their shareholders. Not board members; they're only doing what attorneys and asset advisors instruct them is prudent. Certainly not the asset managers, who are obligated to serve clients above all.

The moral language of protection provides an ideal alibi for the damage inflicted by the pursuit of wealth, to which the players of power piously turn a blind eye. Sorry, hands are tied.

A New Hiding Place for Greed

The fact that some of these players are becoming fabulously, inordinately, obscenely rich is simply a side effect, we're led to believe. And here we find something else tucked behind the shield of fiduciary duty: a new face of greed, vastly larger than the old face of greed. We know that the corporate world is rife with plunder, as tech company billionaires and corporate CEOs make out like bandits. When ProPublica looked at America's four hundred highest earners, tech founders were way up there—people like Larry Ellison, founder of Oracle, and Jan Koum, cofounder of WhatsApp. But *far more numerous* among the four hundred were hedge fund managers. The top ten earners included hedge fund executives like Ken Griffin, founder of Citadel, and Jeffrey Yass, cofounder of Susquehanna International Group.[1]

Wait. Susquehanna International Group? Who's ever heard of this hedge fund or this guy, making $1.3 billion *a year*? If this makes you stop and wonder what's going on, note well: hedge funds were the *largest group identified* in the study, making up about one-fifth of the four hundred top earners. Also numerous were private equity managers. CEOs at the one hundred largest US companies were toddlers compared to these guys; corporate CEOs make a median income of "only" $20 million a year. Yet Stephen Schwarzman, cofounder of the behemoth private equity firm Blackstone, enjoys an average yearly income of $782 million. Close to $1 billion rolling in, *each year*.[2]

Where greed is hiding today most easily, and most massively, is in finance—camouflaged by the cloak of fiduciary duty. A vast shift has occurred that remains little understood.

We know we're long past the world of capitalists like Andrew Carnegie and Cecil Rhodes. Yet we're also beyond the world where corporate CEOs wield the real power. Power has passed to finance. We live in an unheralded new era of asset management capitalism.[3] A world of big capital. The world of fiduciary capitalism.

Wealth today shapes society and the planet with its relentless extraction, yet that wealth—in its anonymized, institutionalized form, which today is its virtually universal form—is governed by fiduciaries. Their duties are now in many ways the ruling force of the system.

Greed Institutionalized at Planetary Scale

If every single tech billionaire, hedge fund manager, and CEO were abducted by aliens tonight, the system would barely notice. It would reconstitute itself with nary a ripple.

The same would happen if aliens abducted every member of every board of directors—the corporate directors, mutual fund directors, pension fund and foundation trustees, all of them. All those menacing "interlocking directorates" that leftists used to fret about back in the day. Forget them.

The matters these directors somberly contemplate are essentially decided before they walk into those walnut-paneled rooms. The seeking of a maximum, limitless, eternal *more* for capital is suffused into the air of those boardrooms like a sleeping gas. It is diffused so widely into the cultural air, the sleepwalking quest has become the business not just of directors but of the global economy.

If the wealth of a single billionaire is impossible for most of us mortals to comprehend, the wealth in the asset management system beggars the imagination.

The mutual funds registered in the US that hold $27 trillion of our common assets are all bound by fiduciary duties. So too are traditional government pension plans—federal, state, and local—which hold some $13 trillion in assets, upon which firefighters and teachers rely. When high-net-worth individuals place assets with wealth managers like the leviathan BlackRock ($10 trillion assets under management, or AUM) or Vanguard ($8 trillion AUM), those relationships are fiduciary in nature. Trustees of foundation and university endowments are fiduciaries of hundreds of billions of assets. Managers of private equity funds, hedge funds, and venture capital funds are all bound by fiduciary duties.[4]

This world of financial assets that is now five times the size of GDP—churning and churning, endlessly extracting—is controlled by a dial that turns only one way, toward *more*. We're told, and we believe, that the single moral obligation of the directors overseeing this vast machine is *never to touch that dial*. Leave it to the experts. Your hands are tied.

Now, take a breath (or a slug of Scotch). Let's consider what this means.

The Terror of a World Built on Fiduciary Duty

What's missing from this picture? *Who* is missing? Again imperialism provides an illuminating analogy. As Edward Said observed, theories of "proper order, good behavior, moral values" not only validate our world, they devalue other worlds.[5] So it was that Teddy Roosevelt could wax eloquent about the manly need of the English race to settle the rugged American West, without a thought to the Native Americans bloodied and massacred as they were hounded out of ancestral homelands.

Bias conceals those it excludes. They're vanished from the imagination—sometimes out of malice, more often out of blindness.

The implicit bias at work misses an obvious truth: when the obligation to capital is the *first* obligation of directors, in effect it becomes the *only* obligation. Any other interest must fit itself within that frame. Social and ecological concerns may be given weight only when they serve the interests of capital.

It is when we view the system from the underside—from the view of the powerless and dispossessed—that we begin to see the terror in a world built on fiduciary duty.

Martin Luther King Jr. spoke of "the 'thingification' of the negro" that occurred in the property system of slavery.[6] In the property system of fiduciary duty, capital bias thingifies the world; this mindset transforms whatever it can into an object for extraction.

In this, our finance system is indeed a worthy heir of imperialism, where entire nations were transformed into things, objects, possessions of the wealthy of Europe. John Stuart Mill, a founding theorist of Western property norms, articulated the underlying property philosophy of empire this way in his *Principles of Political Economy*:

> These [outlying possessions of ours] are hardly to be looked upon as countries ... but more properly as outlying agricultural or manufacturing estates belonging to a larger community. Our West Indian colonies, for example, cannot be regarded as countries with a productive capital of their own ... [but are rather] the place where England finds it convenient to carry on the production of sugar, coffee and a few other tropical commodities.[7]

Mill is considered a classical liberal, known for advocating individual rights and actions that do the greatest good for the greatest number. Still, he wrote, "The sacred duties which civilized nations owe to the independence and nationality of each other, are not binding towards those to whom nationality and independence are certain evil, or at best a questionable good." He assumed the backwardness of nations of color, recommending that India not be given independence.[8]

Obligations binding on one front were not binding on another.[9] The genteel norms of the European landed class did not apply to the dark heathen abroad, nor to the unpropertied, unwashed masses at home.

In our day, the obligations of loyalty and care due to asset holders are not afforded to workers or the environment. Amazon spent $4 million to block the voice of workers at its Staten Island warehouse when Chris Smalls succeeded in organizing a union there. In multiple anti-union meetings, the company called the organizers "thugs." When organizers dropped off food and union materials, Amazon had them arrested for trespassing.[10]

Even when worker rights are hard won, such as wage and hour laws, these protections are circumvented as corporations pursue shareholder profits by sending jobs to low-wage nations. Virtually all major American clothing retailers, including Walmart, Calvin Klein, and Gap, have happily sourced garments from subcontractors in places like Honduras, where low-wage workers labor in export processing zones (EPZs), with factories humming behind walls topped by razor wire, as guards stand sentinel with guns. "The EPZ is an extraction unit," the *Guardian* wrote, "just like the sugar plantations or bauxite mines that came before it." EPZs throughout the Caribbean—pushed by the World Bank and the International Monetary Fund—are colonialism in modern guise.[11]

Extraction of a different sort—extracting the ability of the ocean to support life—occurred as chemical manufacturers evaded US Superfund liability by sending production to less regulated places such as Asia so that shareholders could profit from the largely unregulated, low-cost dumping of hundreds of millions of gallons of untreated toxic chemical waste directly into waters that teem with life (or once did).

This is not the corporate war on nature, nor the evasion of human rights, nor the colonization of the globe by profit-maximizing lords of humankind; no, this is the pursuit of the sacred obligation of fiduciary duty to safeguard other people's money.

The Hushed Heart of the Temple

Fiduciary duty pretends to necessity because it is a legal obligation. Yet when we see other legal obligations callously evaded by corporations and by capital while directors seem not to bat an eye, this offers us a clue. Something other than legality is operating, something more profound than sympathy, deeper even than bias. Something numinous. A *reverence* close to awe.

The tranquil boardrooms of fiduciaries overseeing tens of trillions in assets are hushed places where one walks quietly, speaking in solemn tones, so as not to disturb the deity of wealth. It is a world, not incidentally, where white men hold power; of all US assets under management, 98.6 percent are managed by firms owned by white men.[12] Fiduciary duties are the only area of the economy where these sober men in sober clothes will be found uttering the word "sacred."

Consider, for example, a *Stanford Law Review* article published not long ago by professors from Harvard and Northwestern University. Discussing the duties of boards overseeing pension funds and portfolios of other people's money, they wrote that such board members are "subject to a *sacred trust* [emphasis added] known in the law as fiduciary duty."[13]

Another context where one encounters a tone of absolutism is with corporate fiduciary duties. When a large corporation was urged to set up testing during the pandemic, a senior executive told an activist, "I'm not thinking about the public health benefits. My obligation is to our shareholders."[14] The invocation is final—an incantation intended to end conversation about any other potential obligations.

Ending such conversations was certainly the aim of the law professors. Their article was about how to reconcile so-called ESG investing with fiduciary duty. The authors wrote that directors must act in the sole interest of beneficiaries, which makes it a violation of fiduciary duty to aim for "collateral benefit for third parties." ESG investing is permissible, they concluded, only when it serves beneficiaries directly by "improving risk-adjusted return"—in other words, when it delivers that limitless *more* for capital.[15]

One does not hear CEOs invoke a sacred obligation to pay workers fairly for the wealth they create, nor a moral obligation to protect the ecosystems on which all life depends, nor a patriotic duty to pay the taxes that enable our democratic communities to thrive. These ethical obligations are abrogated by any means possible. The primary moral duty the capitalist system internalizes as its own is the duty to wealth, to capital.

Here's how one massive fiduciary—State Street, a financial services and bank holding company with $4.1 trillion AUM[16]—matter-of-factly explains this stance. Cyrus Taraporevala, CEO of State Street Global Advisors, the investment management arm of State

Street Corporation, emphasized in an interview that the company's commitment is to "value, not values":

> And this is a difficult one because we all do have values. We'd love to espouse them, but when it comes to other people's money, which we are the fiduciary for, we have to ask ourselves, how does this drive value? How does it either increase the returns or mitigate the risk? That is our North Star.[17]

What might those tiny little "values" be? Internationally recognized norms of human rights like the right to join a trade union?[18] Preservation of the global climate on which all life depends? Avoiding tens of thousands of pandemic deaths? Such "collateral benefit[s] for third parties," we are sternly warned by the law professors, must never interfere with the serious business at hand: keeping that dial turned toward risk-adjusted *more*.

The Contract of Eternal Society

If we inquire why fiduciary duties evoke a kind of awe, the reason seems to be that in the Western tradition, property rights are considered sacred. Property rights are the deep, untouchable source of conservative power—the sanctuary of law and tradition that for millennia protected the monarchy and aristocracy, the sanctuary of fiduciary duty where the Stephen Schwarzmans of our time stand as high priests.

In the eighteenth century, Edmund Burke valorized the social order where the propertied class holds highest place, for as he put it, "the property of the nation is the nation." The power to perpetuate property is "that which tends the most to the perpetuation of society itself." This social order is protected, he wrote, by "the great primeval contract of eternal society" that binds posterity "to the end of time." Retain a "potent monarchy" and a "spirited nobility," Burke wrote, and you will have "a protected, satisfied, laborious, and obedient people."[19]

The laws of property Burke revered were harsh. A peasant caught stealing a sheep could be executed. Slaves were brutalized and worked to death, children torn from mothers and sold. The poor were held in contempt. In some parishes, paupers were treated as livestock, twenty men drawing wagons while harnessed together.[20] Property in that world, said British legal theorist William Blackstone, conferred on the owner "sole and despotic dominion."[21] A terrifying phrase if ever there was one.

Today, the monarchy is largely gone. What remains of Burke's world is its notion of property.

If we feel a kind of confusion, disorientation, and fear around questioning the rules of fiduciary duty—a fog of miasma, where change feels murky, impossible, unwise—it is a signal we have entered the predemocratic mind. It is a mind where political judgments are disguised, submerged. "Value, not values." It is a world not designed to be changed. An eternal social order we are severely warned against questioning.

A New Enlightenment

In the world of property, the lot of the majority of us is one of subordination, inferiority, and enforced silence. This is our intended role, as laborious and obedient people. Remarkably, this acquiescence extends often to directors themselves—even to wealthy investors, who often feel intimidated into silence.

That silence is being broken, more and more, by new theories and interpretations that are beginning to be voiced and find early acceptance.

One of the oldest alternative interpretations of fiduciary duty is that of "universal ownership," a term coined in 1995 by Nell Minow and Bob Monks, who observed that institutional investors own such a broad range of assets that they effectively own the economy. "When you own everything, you don't want everything to go to hell"—that's how *ImpactAlpha* described this "emerging doctrine" in a recent story, observing how this view was finding increasing uptake. Among its adherents are people like Hiro Mizuno, until recently chief investment officer for Japan's Government Pension Investment Fund, which has $1.75 trillion in assets.[22]

Another influential theory, articulated by corporate governance scholars Margaret Blair and the late Lynn Stout, is the concept of *team production*. They argue that shareholders do not in fact own corporations but only their shares. Directors' obligation is to the corporation as a whole. And because multiple parties—including shareholders and employees—together produce profits, directors owe a fiduciary duty to these multiple parties, not simply to one party. The view has drawn wide attention among corporate governance scholars.[23]

In *The Shareholder Value Myth*, Cornell law professor Stout witheringly dispatched the common misperception that corporate directors are obligated to maximize gains to shareholders: "Contrary to what many believe, US corporate law does not impose any enforceable legal duty on corporate directors or executives of public corporations to maximize profits or share price."[24]

Let that sink in for a moment: fiduciary duty does not require corporate directors to maximize gains for shareholders—*"contrary to what many believe."*

A still larger rethinking is the emerging view of "intergenerational" fiduciary duties, which builds on the concept of intergenerational equity articulated in international conventions, such as the UN Brundtland Commission Report (1987), which famously defined sustainable development, and the Paris Agreement on climate change (2015).[25]

In this line of thinking, Arjya Majumdar of Jindal Global Law School in Delhi argues that since corporations have perpetual life, directors have a duty to preserve the corporation for future shareholders. This requires the preservation of natural resources on which corporations depend.[26]

The evolution of directors' duties is happening not only in theory but in law. In Europe in particular, new legislation enacted or in the pipeline for the European Union aims to set standards for corporations to require effective protection of the environment and human rights.[27]

Yet while there are stirrings of hope, change often fails to go deep enough, fails to challenge the core rights of capital. Consider the limited way progress often articulates itself. The powerful Mizuno in Japan, who is one of the most vocal advocates for the theory of universal ownership, has organized other institutional investors to pressure asset managers like State Street to manage the "negative externalities" created by the companies they invest in. Urging such activity, he argued, "We want to make sure the capital market is sustainable for the long term."[28] As though the highest goal is preserving capital markets. Sigh.

Capital in Service to Real People

What if we began from a different place? What if we stopped talking about preserving capital markets and turned the question around: *What is the purpose of capital in the real world?* What if we stood with regular people, the excluded, the dispossessed, and asked what they need and how capital can be of service to them?

Regular people like Randy B. of Spencer, Massachusetts, who was struggling with his mortgage when his wife was diagnosed with a rare form of Parkinson's disease and bills were piling up. Investors used capital to aid him, through BlueHub of Boston, a large and successful CDFI with more than $1 billion in AUM chartered to serve the disadvantaged. BlueHub bought Randy's mortgage and negotiated with his lender. It sold the home back to Randy, with a mortgage he could afford, where the principal on his loan was reduced.[29]

In more than one thousand cases like this, BlueHub has helped families avoid foreclosure, with principal balances reduced typically between 28 and 38 percent. Since 2009, when this Stabilizing Urban Neighborhoods (SUN) Initiative was launched in the teeth of the mortgage meltdown, families have retained $100 million in equity that would have otherwise been extracted from them by big capital. These were people in the final stages of foreclosure, close to eviction, who had already lost the titles to their homes. The initiative has been so successful in Massachusetts, it's been rolled out in eleven states.[30]

Investors in the SUN program make annual returns of around 2 to 3 percent, with low risk. Their *purpose* is not maximizing gains, but aiding the disadvantaged, enabling lives of dignity, while receiving reasonable returns. This is what prudent investing in a democratic economy looks like. Unlike philanthropic dollars, investor dollars used in the SUN program are repaid and thus recycled over and over again, amplifying their impact over time.

In terms of system design, the SUN program is a new architecture built around a living *purpose*, its rollout to multiple states representing a new *infrastructure* in formation. It isn't perfect. It's not Santa Claus. While homeowners enjoy principal reduction, they're also required to share some appreciation of their home's price with the lender. Some borrowers in the program have found that unfair and sued.[31]

Still, BlueHub is an organization I admire, and the principle at work here seems the right one. If we had a democratic economy, this is how the entire 2008 meltdown could have been handled—all the genius and might of finance deployed on behalf of we the people.

7

THE UNSEEN UNDERSIDE
OF WEALTH

It's About Extracting from the Rest of Us

THE PRISTINE, SANITIZED, REVERENT world of wealth—its need to be perpetually maximized, to have its risks minimized, to be universally protected through fiduciary duty—all of this is a self-referential system that perceives its rules and customs as morally right. It is a system so focused on benefit to wealth that it becomes blind to impact on others.

The underside of "wealth creation" is that it often involves excess extraction from others. Here's how it works.

We think of wealth as a pile of money, like a stash of gold. But that's not how it functions in the era of asset management capitalism. Wealth is invested. It becomes capital, money that must limitlessly grow. Investments are about staking claims, finding places to put capital that will allow it to become bigger, to yield a return.

Financial assets function as *claims and obligations*. Every asset held by one person is a claim against someone else. A house is a real thing; a mortgage is a claim against its value, an obligation owed by the homeowner to the bank, and indirectly to the bank's shareholders. A municipal bond is a claim on the tax income of a city. A share of stock is a claim on the value of a company. Credit card debt is a claim against your checkbook.

If our system were functioning normally, as it did decades ago, these claims would be manageable. Having a mortgage allows us to buy a home when we lack the assets to pay for it in advance. All good. But wait.

As we saw in chapter 2, financial assets today have swollen far beyond normal size. The world today is awash in financial capital, the liquid, contemporary version of property. In our property regime, this means the system's center of gravity has shifted away from the real economy of homes and small companies and jobs, and moved up into the sphere of finance. The power of that world, the world of wealth and the wealthy, has increased. Its extraction from the rest of us has grown dramatically.

We're the Donkey the Wealthy Are Riding

This state of affairs is apparent when we look at financial assets in aggregate, at the system level. In 2021, the stock market reached 205 percent of US economic output.[1] The same year, global debt reached more than 350 percent of global GDP.[2] In early 2022, according to the US Federal Reserve, total domestic financial assets stood at five times GDP.[3]

If you now feel like laying your head on a pillow and dozing, wait. Bear with me as I unpack these numbers.

GDP represents the real economy, the world of jobs and purchasing, all the flows of income and spending. Sitting atop this real economy is the sphere of finance, the world of capital, which in the US is now *five times* the size of the real economy (refer back to figure 2.1). This matters. This, in fact, *hurts*—because it means the wealthy are placing more and more onerous claims on the rest of us. We're paying more and more (or losing more and more) to keep their wealth growing. We're the donkey the wealthy are riding.

Though often missing in the everyday discourse, financialization has been widely studied by many economists for decades. Even a group of economists at the International Monetary Fund has recognized its pernicious effect, with their body of research known as "Too Much Finance."[4]

As economists Dirk Bezemer, Michael Hudson, and Howard Reed explain in a recent analysis commissioned by the organization where I work, the Democracy Collaborative, financialization is the diversion of financial flows away from production and consumption and toward asset markets. It means the system is now less about manufacturing stuff and more about manufacturing debt. Finance once was in service to communities, jobs, homes, family firms—making loans to small businesses, helping people buy houses, and so on. Now we're in service to finance. Instead of having an economy designed to produce more value in the real world, for regular people, the economy's machinery has been rejiggered to produce higher asset valuations.[5]

Finance warps the system's function away from usefulness in the real world—away from innovation, productivity growth, and widely shared income. Instead, as Bezemer and his colleagues put it, the asset becomes the basis of the economic system. The resulting revenue flows benefit the few.[6] That minority—the wealthy and the financial industry that serves them—comes to dominate society.[7]

In this state of affairs, extraction revs into overdrive. System relationships shift out of balance—most of us left owing, while a few collect the bounty.

Much of the wealth of the 1 percent is debt owed by households and by governments.[8]

That means, as our society watches the wealth of multimillionaires and billionaires magically expand as though out of thin air, much of that wealth is being extracted from the pockets of ordinary people and our taxpayer-financed governments. We're painfully foregoing other spending options in order to pay the 1 percent.[9]

Financial assets have become a burden, a giant sucking action squeezing consumer pocketbooks, creating unemployment, pushing housing prices to unreachable heights, creating monopolies that hobble family businesses, blocking our ability to tackle climate change, destabilizing the economy with stock market booms and busts. And enabling billionaires to capture democracy.[10]

In *Capital in the Twenty-First Century*, Thomas Piketty documented that the swelling income of the wealthy results in growing inequality for most everyone else. If economic growth is, say, around 2 or 3 percent, while capital seeks to grow at 5 or 7 percent, the wealthy increase their income by extracting from others, through methods such as reducing income to labor. If my slice of the pie is growing much faster than the whole pie is growing, then your slice is getting smaller. Piketty showed this to be the truth of capitalism over two hundred years.[11]

Today it's true on steroids. The finance, insurance, and real estate (FIRE) sector is now the locus where inequality is being created.[12]

It's accelerated massively in *just two years*. Amid recent crises—the COVID pandemic, followed by inflation in food and fuel costs—the wealth of the world's ten richest men doubled. The incomes of 99 percent of humanity fell. The wealthiest *ten people* now own more wealth than 40 percent of all humanity.[13]

If the growing wealth of the few is something we see and talk about, the aggregate, systemic problem of financialization remains largely outside the public discourse. We'll look more deeply at the results of financialization in coming chapters. Suffice it to say here that the truth of it is unsettling: finance is sapping society's resilience. And the impact is hitting most of us—including workers, including the natural order, including democracy.

8

WORKERS ARE NOT MEMBERS OF THE CORPORATION

The Myths of Corporate Governance and the Income Statement

IT'S WORTH ASKING: What's missing from the airtight world of maximizing and fiduciary duty? *Who* is missing? Who is vanished from the imagination?

The first group that springs to mind is labor. Workers. Regular people who go to work every day and do the work of the economy. When we turn our gaze to this largely dispossessed group, we see how obligations binding on one front are not binding on another, how the rights and privileges enjoyed by capital are not enjoyed by workers.

The reason is that we buy into the myth of how corporations are governed.

THE MYTH OF CORPORATE GOVERNANCE

Workers are not members of corporations. Membership is reserved for capital owners, while workers are disenfranchised and dispossessed.

At the deepest, unconscious level, this myth is based on the idea that corporations are objects whose *ownership* is held by shareholders—a picture that gives rise to a conception of how corporations should be governed.

When we stop to look at this picture, it's odd. What companies are, self-evidently, is human communities. A pile of capital by itself creates nothing. Human labor sets all the wheels spinning. It's workers who *are* the company.

But in the world of boardrooms, we encounter a curious reversal of reality. Those people walking around *being* a company, creating its products, doing its work, answering the phone—they're outsiders. The phantom algorithms possessing shares of stock for a few minutes, or the massive funds holding slices of everything through multiple layers of intermediaries—they're the insiders. The business media considers this a reasonable picture of reality, even as most shareholders never set foot in "their" companies and often do not know the names of companies they "own."

If You Want to Vote, Get Rich

At work is implicit bias against workers. Where this is held in place is in the design of corporate *governance*. Corporate boards are elected solely by the capital interests who hold shares. And those boards stand invisibly over CEOs, possessing the power to hire, fire, and compensate CEOs. Maximizing income to capital is the moral heart of the corporation, its sole *purpose*. So we're told.

This is the worldview of property, holding archaic assumptions dear to Edmund Burke. It's a world where only those who possess or control wealth matter—and the more wealth you have, the more you matter, hence the more votes you have in corporate governance. The lot of workers is one of subordination and enforced silence.

We take for granted the ways economic power is reserved for capital. We see it as normal. Just as society once considered it normal that suffrage was limited to men of property. As the French minister

Francois Guizot once proclaimed, if people wanted to vote, they should get rich.[1]

Privilege in the predemocratic world intertwined bias based on race, sex, and property. Of the three, only property bias, capital bias, today remains legal—indeed, mandatory.

We're told it's "market forces" that set wages. Yet markets cannot function without information, and wage information is massively missing. Corporations deem wage data "proprietary" information, which means the price of labor is private property (!). I once was tasked by the Rockefeller Foundation with yearlong research into the status of workers in food and agriculture, and while I and a research associate searched for months, the only wage data we could find was years out of date, and available solely in the aggregate.[2]

If financial markets experienced such a black hole of information, they couldn't function. They would fall prey to manipulation by those with power—as have labor markets.

Making the Invisible Visible

To help break the trance of the normality of it all, imagine for a moment that the prices of stocks were set as wages now are. Imagine that workers enjoy the position in boardrooms that capital now enjoys.

Shareholders wishing to sell stock would be shown into a room and offered a price, which they could take or leave. They would have zero information about what other shareholders received yesterday, or what shareholders at other companies were receiving for comparable stock. If shareholders sought collective power through mutual funds, they would be fought by companies. Workers, on the other hand, would automatically enjoy collective advantage through unions. Only workers would have a vote for the corporation's governing body. Maximizing gains to workers would be the purpose of the corporation, taught in business schools, upheld in the courts, tracked daily in the press. If shareholders were unhappy with their earnings, they'd be told they could sell their shares and invest elsewhere. They'd be advised to seek retraining in how to invest.

Beyond boardrooms, antiworker bias is reflected in the cultural discourse, where worker well-being is often treated perfunctorily. The single measure that policy makers and journalists tend to point to is "unemployment," implying that workers are fine if they're "employed," even if it's part-time work with no benefits. With investments, we don't say X percent of funds are "invested," end of story. No, we track performance minute by minute.

Even unemployment figures themselves are inadequate, gamed to hide the reality of how many are out of work or struggling. The US Bureau of Labor Statistics counts people as unemployed only if they've been actively looking for work over the last *four weeks*. The long-term unemployed—including those so discouraged they've stopped looking—are invisible in unemployment figures.

Pundits note often how US workers' wages, after accounting for inflation, have been essentially flat for forty years (with some recent upticks).[3] It's common to point to the role of policy in this—President Ronald Reagan firing the air traffic controllers, the failures of policy makers to adequately raise the minimum wage or to make it easier to join unions. Less often noted is how a propensity to depress worker income is designed into our property regime. When policy makers deregulate or when corporations send operations overseas (which amounts to the same thing), they're setting loose the workings of the capitalist machine in pure form: the machine designed to produce a growing stream of earnings for capital, like ball bearings off an assembly line.

Capital Pockets Wealth That Workers Create

When capital seeks its endless increase of income, it's protected by fiduciary duty and by the power of capital in corporate governance.

When workers seek an increase of income, they're treated as the enemy. Antiworker bias is silently expressed—and set in motion—in the design of the income statement: the scorecard by which companies define and track success, the structure of *accountability* for managers.

This standard financial statement may be Greek to many of us, but it's worth understanding because it's the universal lens through which all companies view their activity. In its stripped-down form, it's this simple equation:

Revenue – expenses = profit

Hidden here is capital bias. The wondrous word *profit* speaks reverently to the aim beyond all aims, the "bottom line": maximizing income to capital.[4] On the other hand, income to labor—*expense*—is very, very bad; expenses by their nature are to be driven down.

THE MYTH OF THE INCOME STATEMENT

Income to capital ("profit") is always to be increased, while income to labor ("expense") is always to be decreased. These are implicit rules of the income statement.

The upshot of this structural bias against workers (surprise!) is that absentee capital pockets the wealth workers create. McKinsey Global Institute documented this in a recent study, looking at where each dollar of company revenue went for large corporations (with more than $1 billion in revenues), among thirty-seven nations of the Organization of Economic Cooperation and Development (OECD). After revenue flowed into a company, where did that money go? Who received that income? Over the past twenty-five years, the study documented a two-thirds increase in capital income, along with a 6 percent decrease in labor income. This was at a time when worker productivity was substantially increasing. As McKinsey (need I add: not a Marxist organization) summed up its findings, "gains from labor productivity went predominantly to capital income."[5]

It bears repeating: capital is pocketing the wealth that workers create. Yet it's all merely technical, we're told.

Consider, for example, when Salesforce laid off one thousand people. "We're reallocating resources to position the company for continued growth," a spokesperson said silkily. The company was "eliminating some positions that no longer map to our business priorities." Nothing in there about how the company was already substantially profitable. No thought as to how periods of unemployment derail lives, reduce lifetime income, and create immense hardship for families.

The very banality of the language obscures the cruelty of what's occurring: that income to labor is being eliminated so as to increase income to capital.

The War on Workers

Beneath the silky language is a stark fact: capital is at war against workers. And it's winning that war.

Driving down labor income is often critical to maximizing capital income, since labor costs are generally the largest portion of corporate "expenses." Yet this systemic bias is taken for granted. There are economists who see this and speak of it—for example, James Galbraith, who has written of "the predatory attack on unions and labor."[6] There are nonprofits who work to make this attack visible, like the Economic Policy Institute. And there are magazines that write about it, like the wonderful *Dollars and Sense* and *Jacobin*. But what's remarkable is how rarely most of us seem to notice what's going on.

The "decline of unions" tends to be spoken of in passive voice, as though those outdated, useless unions were something people just lost interest in. We don't notice how absurd it is that workers have to organize one shop at a time, when Starbucks has 8,800 shops, while in corporate governance, capital is automatically and universally empowered, not a single fight required.[7]

We don't hear outrage that, as corporations fight workers attempting to join unions, they're fighting a human right. Imagine if Starbucks fought to keep Black people from finding voice in the workforce, or insisted women be kept silent. Such moves would meet with universal uproar, because race and gender bias are culturally illegitimate. Anti-worker bias is normal. Acceptable.

Driving Labor Out of the Economy

This bias is frightening in its sweep. Capital is driving labor income, and labor itself, out of the economy.

Today there are one hundred million working-age Americans not in the labor force.[8] Just 62.2 percent of working-age people are working, down from a peak of 67.3 two decades ago (see figure 8.1).[9] Yet even that figure—the labor force participation rate—is misleading. The US Bureau of Labor Statistics counts someone as "in the labor force" *if they did any work at all for pay in the surveyed week.* Delivered a few pizzas for UberEats? You're in the labor force. Had a one-time graphic design project, then zip the rest of the year? You're in the labor force.[10]

Among the diminishing number "in the labor force," a dwindling proportion of workers enjoy the traditional full-time jobs of yore. Insecure, unstable, contingent work, as we have seen, is estimated by the Government Accountability Office (GAO) to be a terrifying 40 percent of the "labor force." I emphasize *estimated*, because when I dug into footnotes, I found disagreement, year to year, even on the definition of contingent work.[11]

The destruction of reliable jobs is a history-shaping trend. The rage it creates is driving the white working class into the arms of the right. The very notion of steady, family-supporting work is disintegrating. Yet the capsized vessel of labor is barely on our radar—a shadow out there that blinks into view now and then, mostly absent from the public imagination.

It's poised to become worse, as automation takes over. If the processes of job destruction are accelerating in our time, the propensity to treat workers as the enemy is as old as Andrew Carnegie shooting steelworkers. The marching orders are there in the income statement: maximize income to capital, minimize income to labor. The antiworker bias is embedded in the governance of corporations, which gives workers no voice in the decisions that shape their lives.

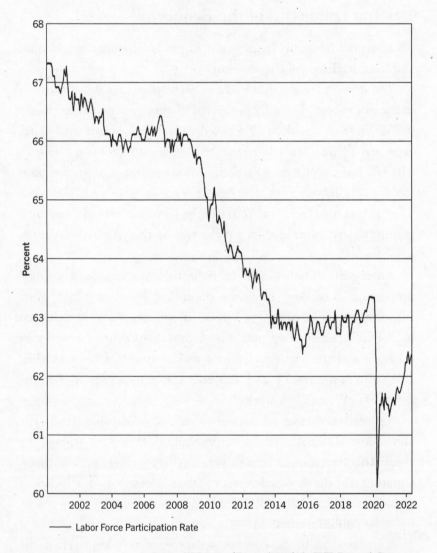

Source: US Bureau of Economic Analysis, FRED Economic Data,
St. Louis Federal Reserve, https://fred.stlouisfed.org/series/CIVPART.

FIGURE 8.1: Plummeting labor force participation 2000–2022

The capital bias at work echoes the male bias of the 1800s, when a woman had no right to own property and, as Elizabeth Cady Stanton asserted in the Seneca Falls Declaration of 1848, was compelled "to submit to laws, in the formation of which she had no voice." Upon marriage, as Stanton put it, a woman became "civilly dead." Today, when you take a job with a corporation, in the governing structure of that corporate society, you become civilly dead.

Dispensing with Employees Altogether

In Europe, the situation is less bleak. The old-fashioned, high-wage, unionized form of labor relations retains more clout in places like Germany, Norway, and Sweden, where codetermination laws support widespread worker representation and strong collective bargaining agreements, giving workers a voice in corporate governance. The power of labor is under pressure, but in many ways intact.

In the US, labor power is seeing a remarkable and hopeful resurgence. But as hopeful as this is, labor is unlikely to become the primary force for progressive change it once was. A key reason: it's not just unions that have been dismantled, it's employment itself.

Consider the story the *Wall Street Journal* ran a few years back, carrying the chilling title "The End of Employees." As the *Journal* reported, "never before have American companies tried so hard to employ so few people." This article from 2017 was tracking a trend then gaining steam across industries, which the *Journal* called "subcontracting." I call it the rise of throwaway workers. People unloading shipping containers at Walmart no longer worked for Walmart, but for a trucking company, which in turn subcontracted with temporary staffing agencies. *Half* the workers at Google didn't work for Google but were subcontractors.[12]

Places like UberEats, DoorDash, and TaskRabbit weren't yet the major force they would become, disaggregating work further, turning jobs into discrete units of small tasks. But subcontracting was one more piece of what has become the new normal: give workers no security, few benefits like health insurance and retirement, virtually no opportunities for advancement, and little in the way of belonging or being part of a work community. Instead, offer a daily diet of insecurity, uncertainty, instability, and fear.

Contracting is often seen as a stopgap, the *Journal* continued, "until more jobs are automated, freeing firms to dispense with some workers altogether." Within ten years, consulting firm Accenture predicted, one company—among the largest in the world—will have "no full-time employees outside of the C-suite."[13]

Now, pause a moment to consider this aim, so casually mentioned: *dispensing with workers altogether*. Note the low-key, placid way this ghastly goal is voiced. This is bias at work. It tells us that the systematic degradation of work and workers is something our culture considers so ho-hum as to merit mere casual mention.

The Detritus of Lives Damaged

Dehumanizing language leads to dehumanizing treatment. Dehumanizing treatment creates suffering. After the war on workers took off in the 1980s, millions who lost work turned to opioids, later to heroin. Millions who once held good manufacturing jobs didn't work again. As research shows, families that suffer unemployment and loss of income tend to see an increase in dysfunction in the form of substance abuse, domestic violence, depression, and declining marriage rates—metastasizing into the next generation, as the children of the unemployed experience mental health problems.[14]

Minimizing income to labor leaves tragedy in its wake. This tragedy is a direct outcome of maximizing income to capital.

Look back to the beginning of the 1980s bull market in stocks, and one finds Margaret Thatcher in the UK deregulating the London Stock Exchange and selling off state assets,[15] with Reagan in the US declaring "morning in America"—beginning the shift to deregulation, tax cuts, and privatization that would help jumpstart long-depressed stock markets.[16]

The rising gains to capital that appeared were fueled to a large extent by cuts to labor's income. Between 1980 and 2000, 2 million manufacturing jobs in the US were vaporized—with an even larger 5.5 million lost between 2000 and 2017.[17] A shrinking share of the nation's income went to labor. Over the three decades following 1980, labor's share of US gross domestic income experienced a drop of 12 percent.[18]

Neoliberal policies set the capital extraction machine loose, yet that machine was already internally designed to decrease income to labor in order to increase income to capital. That's how the system is supposed to work—according to the myth of the income statement, the myth of maximizing, the myth of fiduciary duty. Lo and behold, it's how it did work (see figure 8.2).

Inside companies, the rising pressure to keep delivering the profits/earnings that the stock market demanded, even as top lines of revenue struggled to grow fast enough, meant pesky "expenses" had to be continually pared back. The 1980s was when massive layoffs first became standard practice, ushered in famously by "Neutron Jack" Welch of General Electric, known for his neutron bomb–like practices of destroying people while leaving buildings intact. As he closed factories and fired workers by the tens of thousands, Welch turned GE into the most valuable company in the world, paving the path toward how companies now conventionally operate. Mass layoffs, outsourcing, and offshoring all became common practice, as did stratospheric CEO pay and a stock market climbing ever upward for years. Little noted in the business and financial press was the landscape littered with the detritus of lives damaged and a working class destabilized.[19]

Extraction on Autopilot, in Overdrive

One worker whose life was pulled under in the downdraft was Shannon Mulcahy, a worker at Rexnord, a ball bearing factory in Indianapolis that was moved to Mexico in 2016 (the layoff of three hundred workers was something Trump tweeted about, uselessly, "No more!"). As someone who'd grown up in a manufactured housing community,

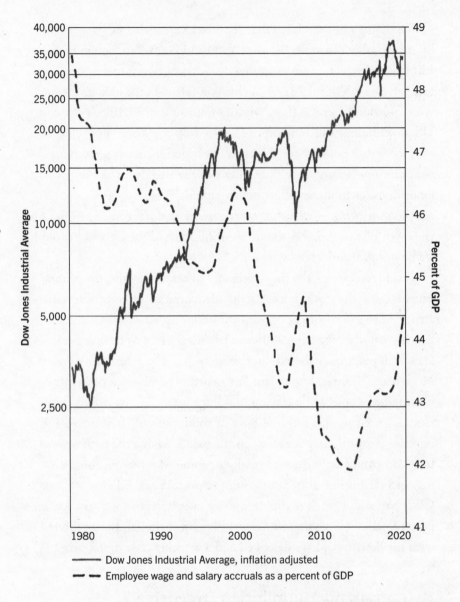

Sources: US Bureau of Economic Analysis, St. Louis Federal Reserve; Macrotrends.net.

FIGURE 8.2: The fall of wages drives the rise of Dow, 1980–2020

Shannon found in her factory job an opportunity to escape an abusive relationship and, later, to help pay medical bills for a disabled grandchild. As she trained her replacement at Rexnord, she spoke with a Mexican worker, Ricardo, and they discovered he would be paid one-sixteenth of her salary. (Note the haphazard way wage information comes to light.)

Like most workers formerly in manufacturing, Shannon would not again enjoy her previous level of wages. She struggled to find new work. She struggled also to understand who was responsible for derailing her life, as she sought to find who owned the Rexnord plant.

The plant had been owned by a British conglomerate, which sold it to a private equity (PE) firm, the Carlyle Group. Carlyle then sold it to another private equity group, which used the asset value of Rexnord to borrow money that was loaded onto the company's back. Then that PE firm sold the factory to a group of mutual funds. Farah Stockman, who recounted this story in *American Made: What Happens to People When Work Disappears*, concluded, "Shannon never did find the list of shareholders."[20]

In our financialized era, it hardly matters anymore if a ruthless guy like Jack Welch is in the driver's seat. Ruthlessness is a norm, with big capital the new boss. At Rexnord, as the process of financial extraction shifted from PE firm to PE firm to mutual funds, it was maximizing that was in charge, in overdrive. Pedal to the metal. People like Shannon got run over. But it was myths that told us it was all just technical stuff, myths providing the mold of ideas that obscures and forgives such behavior. Who goes to bed angry about the design of corporate governance or the income statement? Who can even find the individuals getting rich off keeping the machine running?

The idea that a corporation is not a human community but an object owned by capital: it's the thingification of the collective human project we call a company. Company-as-object is a potent image in the cultural mind. An invisible force. It normalizes the reckless economy in which companies like Rexnord are sold over and over and over again, with the humans who *are* the company experiencing only one constant: that each new owner will demand greater extraction, throw more bodies under the bus, prioritize payment to capital over payment to workers. This is the system that looks at the ongoing mass destruction of livelihoods and calls it "wealth creation."

9

ECOLOGICAL AND SOCIETAL DAMAGES ARE NOT REAL

The Myth of Materiality

THE GAME MOVES ON.

One of the juicy types of prey in the sights of capital these days is ecological wealth. Hard on the hunt to capture it is private equity. These firms—Carlyle Group, Blackstone, KKR, Cerberus, and the like—can be thought of as the 3.0 version of Cecil Rhodes and Jack Welch. PE firms, and similar forms of private capital like hedge funds, are today the nimblest (read: least regulated, least transparent) and hungriest capital carnivores out there devouring the world's assets.

Unlike the corporate equities (stocks) that trade on public stock markets, private equity is a more hidden world, where only big investors can play. PE funds use other people's money as they buy companies, load them with debt, "cut costs" (read: lay off workers), sell off assets, then flip companies to new buyers, generally in three to seven years. In the process, these companies become twice as likely to go bankrupt as publicly traded companies. As the pandemic unfolded, private equity was behind *more than half* of US corporate defaults. Yet

PE executives were walking away with median annual income of over $100 million each.[1]

In one notorious example, PE owners overloaded Toys R Us with so much debt, it left the firm unable to modernize and drove it into bankruptcy, costing thirty-three thousand workers their jobs. Overall, private equity killed 1.3 million retail jobs in ten years.

It's apt that *Mother Jones* termed private equity the "smash-and-grab economy." It represents a massive new looting phase of capitalism. (The *Onion* quipped in a headline, after the Minneapolis protests following George Floyd's death, "Protestors Criticized for Looting Businesses Without Forming Private Equity Firm First.")

These funds are distressingly popular, with assets swelling from under $1 trillion in 2000 to nearly $10 trillion today.[2]

In observing PE firms, we can witness anew the game of capitalism on the move, changing shape, flowing around barriers we erect, devouring the alternatives we create.

Wage and hour laws? No problem; send jobs overseas, Uberize, automate.

Superfund toxic waste laws? No biggie; send factories to China.

CDFIs doing fair lending in Black neighborhoods? Hey, great: move in and grab the home equity those families accumulated.

Selling Dirty Assets into the Shadows

The latest tale of this relentlessness has to do with climate change. In this story, we see how the apex predator, private equity, has moved in on progressive victories, such as fossil fuel divestment, net zero commitments by oil giants, and pipeline permits blocked.

The result? Well, you already know. It's a sobering tale. Perhaps the better term is *terrifying*.

For years, progressive shareholders and activists have leaned on institutional investors to divest from fossil fuels, and have demanded that the oil industry advance toward climate goals. They've succeeded to a remarkable extent. Some 1,500 institutional investors with more than $40 trillion in assets have committed to fossil fuel divestment—including pension funds of unionized workers like the New York State Teachers Retirement System; universities like Oxford, Cambridge, Harvard, and most of the other Ivies; the Ford Foundation; and the Universities of California and Michigan.[3] Hearing the drumbeat, publicly traded oil firms have set emission reduction goals, cleaning up their act by getting rid of their dirtiest assets.[4]

Guess who's buying those dirty assets? Private equity.

When ConocoPhillips in 2017 sold off its polluting assets in Colorado's San Juan Basin and in New Mexico for $3 billion, the eager buyer on the other end was Hilcorp, backed by the PE giant Carlyle. When BP sold off its dirty Alaska operations for $5.6 billion, the same buyer stood ready. Today the PE-backed Hilcorp stands tall as the biggest known emitter of methane in the US—producing close to 50 percent more emissions than ExxonMobil, even though Hilcorp produces just a third of Exxon's oil and gas volume. Methane matters enormously, accounting for a quarter of today's global warming, as it's more than 25 *times* as potent as carbon dioxide in its ability to trap heat in the atmosphere.[5]

When Royal Dutch Shell sold off its stake in a Nigerian oil field in 2021, it seemed a positive step toward the company's goal of net zero emissions by 2050. Yet the buyer was a PE-backed firm, Trans-Niger Oil & Gas, which apparently cared not a fig for that goal. The result: flaring, the wasteful burning of excess gas, quadrupled. Instead of winding down oil production, Trans-Niger planned to triple it.[6]

PE firm KKR has been out there keeping fracking going strong, expanding its fracking operations by buying all of ConocoPhillips' drilling assets in Wyoming in 2020—doubling down on exploration and production.[7]

And then there's the grassroots success won against the Dakota Access pipeline in North Dakota, after thousands joined the Standing Rock Sioux Tribe to halt the construction of this pipeline on

Indigenous land. In 2020, the tribe won a victory when the courts struck down a key federal permit, a success the Supreme Court upheld in 2022. Sad to say, the pipeline continued to operate without a permit. The punchline: a significant stake in the firm that owns the pipeline is held by Blackstone, the world's largest PE firm.[8]

These are anecdotes in what is a massive, global endeavor by private equity, which since 2010 has invested a jaw-dropping $1.1 trillion in energy deals—double the market value of Exxon, Chevron, and Royal Dutch Shell combined. The great majority of those investments has been in fossil fuels, with only 12 percent in renewable power, according to a study by Pitchbook Data. The upshot is that some of the most irresponsible emitters of greenhouse gases are shifting into the shadows, operating with minimal public scrutiny, with no comprehensive disclosure of either holdings or environmental impact.[9]

Institutional Investors Stampede into Private Equity

At a time when the United Nations is warning it's now or never to limit global warming—a time when we face "unprecedented heat waves, terrifying storms, widespread water shortages and the extinction of a million species of plants and animals," as UN Secretary-General António Guterres has warned—private equity is running hard in the wrong direction. It's pushing the planet toward the storms, the heat waves, the extinctions, because it's following the capital-centric system's prime directive: squeeze every last dime of "wealth" from wherever it can be found.[10] And institutional investors are rushing in the same direction, as they pile eagerly into PE funds.

Institutional investors' stampede into PE funds has been led by workers' money in the form of pension funds, which represent about *half* the money invested with private equity.[11] Also involved are foundations like Ford, which in 2020 held nearly $1 billion in PE investments.[12] And included are public universities, which by definition exist to serve the public interest. Institutional investors like these have been "desperate for access" to flagship PE funds, *Institutional Investor* reported.[13] As one expert put it, institutional capital "is extremely hungry to seek yield."[14]

Harvard's $53 billion endowment in mid-2021 was allocated 34 percent to private equity (and 33 percent to hedge funds).[15] For Princeton, the allocation to private equity in late 2021 was a massive 42 percent of assets. The University of Michigan was also 42 percent in private equity.[16] These institutions have all pledged to divest from fossil fuels. Yet given the opacity of private equity, have fossil fuels slipped into these portfolios unseen? Possibly. Possibly not. What does seem likely is that these institutions were focused on the mouth-watering returns PE funds offered.

Why the Planet Is Missing

This brings us to the obscure notion of materiality.

We've seen how labor is vanished from the imagination in the capital-centric view of things. Who else, what else, is missing?

The list is both short and long: the world, ecology, society—in short, most everything is missing, everything except capital.

THE MYTH OF MATERIALITY

Gains to capital are real ("material"), while social and environmental damages are not real (not material), except to the extent they affect capital. This is among the rules of corporate and financial accounting.

As directors and asset managers go about the business of seeking superlative portfolio performance, they often do not question how investment gains are obtained, particularly when an opaque intermediary like private equity is involved. What Harvard saw in fiscal 2021 was that its PE holdings (including venture capital) posted a gain of

77 percent.[17] This is like the drug high of an addict, so wondrous that it blinds one to the mess of life left all around. The myth of materiality holds this blindness in place.

(By the by, those 77 percent returns are not typical. In the decade up to 2020, private equity's annualized returns were only marginally above—by about one-half of 1 percent—the S&P 500.)[18]

"Materiality," in the real world, means the quality or character of being material, possessing corporeal form. Something you can kick and it will move, or it'll hurt your toe.

One might suppose the planet is material. But no.

In the upside-down, capital-centric world of corporate and financial accounting, materiality means what's important to investors. What's real—often the *only* thing that's real—is the set of numbers that show up in ethereal spreadsheets and financial statements.

The rules of accounting say materiality is about what's important enough to be included in—and what can be omitted from—a financial statement.[19] Implicitly, financial statements are a report to investors as the "owners" of the object that is a corporation. PE funds are pools holding multiple companies—in aggregate, around 110,000 US companies.[20] As these funds report on returns, they are reporting to those our system considers the ultimate owners of these firms, the allocators of capital: institutional investors and wealthy families.

Financial statements give us a picture of reality viewed through the lens of capital. Ergo: what's real is what's real to capital. In system design terms, this is another way in which *accountability* is designed in.

Everything relevant to capital must be included in financial statements. Is there a pending lawsuit that must be disclosed? A product failure that must be revealed? The founder of Theranos went to prison for failing to reveal relevant facts about her blood testing product in development. But is the company doing something that might damage oceans, or degrade local ecosystems, or harm communities?

Not material. Not real. *Unless the issue in question benefits or harms the interests of capital.*

Materiality is an airtight tautology of capital bias.

Destruction of Democracy, School Shootings: Not Material

When the PE-backed Greystar began buying up rental properties across ten states after the Great Recession, what was *not* material to them was that rents soared, trash piled up in hallways, repairs were neglected, security guards appeared less often, and tenants felt less safe. What *was* material, as Greystar founder and CEO Bob Faith bragged, was his ability to squeeze money from buildings—hiking profits from one complex 24 percent in a single year. [21]

Greystar was one among many PE-backed firms that cashed in on the wreckage of the 2008 crisis, snapping up homes at rock-bottom prices and turning them into rentals, after 3.7 million families suffered foreclosure.[22] This trend, driven by private equity, is the financialization of housing—the transformation of housing from a social good into a wealth extraction vehicle for investors. It's a trend not likely mentioned in investment prospectuses.[23]

Then there's the destruction of local newspapers, another trend that isn't material in the accounting, but is material to communities left in the dark. The premier vulture firm in this business is Alden Capital, a hedge fund that now controls more than two hundred newspapers and partners with PE firms in some of its biggest take-overs, which have included the *Chicago Tribune*, *Baltimore Sun*, and *New York Daily News*. The model is simple: cut staff, sell the real estate and rent it back at an inflated price, wring out every dime until the thing lies gasping on the floor and dies. It's of little concern that, when a newspaper vanishes, communities see lower voter turnout, increased polarization, and less civic engagement. The death of news-papers feeds a creeping sickness in democracy. You won't find that in the fine print of PE prospectuses. Not material.[24]

Then there are the school shootings, like Sandy Hook, where private equity profit seeking may have fed youthful derangement. The PE firm Cerberus Capital Management created Remington, maker of the Bushmaster AR-15-style rifle and other firearms, when it bought many smaller gun makers and rolled them into a conglomerate. That firm began aggressive marketing aimed at young men, many of them too young to be lawful purchasers. Among the macho new marketing slogans: "Consider your man card reissued." The Bushmaster AR-15-style rifle appeared in combat video games like *Call of Duty*, the game that the troubled young Adam Lanza played many hours each day, using the Bushmaster to wage war. The Bushmaster was the gun Lanza took into Sandy Hook Elementary School in 2012, when he massacred 20 first graders.[25]

By the time family lawsuits attained a victorious settlement in 2022 (fought by the company all the way to the Supreme Court), Remington had already gone bankrupt. Cerberus had given up its ownership. Did the aggressive behavior by the Cerberus-owned firm trouble institutional investors? Seemingly not. Cerberus (named for the three-headed dog guarding the gates of hell) still succeeds nicely at attracting institutional investments, with its $60 billion in AUM. Bankruptcies happen.[26] The dustup doesn't seem to have been material to the assets of cofounder and CEO Steve Feinberg, whose net worth in two years leapt from $1.5 billion to $2.3 billion.[27]

Sneaking the Planet into Materiality

Responsible investors have beat their head against the brick wall of materiality for decades, arguing for greater disclosure by companies, making the case that social and ecological impacts do matter—yet these activists have mostly been forced to argue that such things matter because they impact investor returns.

There are pioneers seeking to break this open, particularly with ecological issues. There's a movement for "science-based targets" that attempts to turn the paradigm around—to start with the actually material world, the planet, not with portfolios, and require companies to set greenhouse gas emissions targets based on what science tells us the planet's atmosphere can actually absorb.[28]

There are people like Bill Baue, a corporate governance iconoclast I've known since the days of *Business Ethics*, who is now with the decade-old r3.0 initiative, working to institutionalize the paradigm of thresholds—in which we start with the planet's various ecological thresholds, and allocate what companies can do within those thresholds.[29] He's out there regularly critiquing many of the weaker frameworks, like the International Sustainability Standards Board (ISSB); in a public comment letter, for example, Baue said ISSB's approach to sustainability should be labeled "Sociopathic Materiality."[30]

There's even the new concept of "double materiality" that has emerged in recent years, in which companies are to report not only on sustainability issues that are financially material, but also on those material to the market, the environment, and people.[31]

Such thinking represents a much-needed advance. Though I confess it strikes me as backward, that the way to get the planet to show up (the actual, large planet) is by contorting our thinking into the pretzel of *double* materiality.

Can There Be Too Much Profit?

Could we take a more pointed approach?

I once asked a PE executive, do you worry you're making too much profit? He nearly leapt from his shoes. "Well, no one's ever asked me *that* before," he said with a laugh. He was someone using PE-like approaches to convert companies to employee ownership, so I considered him one of the good guys. Still, I imagined he might have gone home that night and told his wife, *You won't believe what someone asked me today.*

Does anyone at Harvard ask, Are portfolio gains too high?

Why do we so rarely ask these questions?

Perhaps it's because only capital and its representatives are in the room where decisions are made. When the disempowered gain voice, bias can be named and defeated.

We're unlikely to see the end of wealth supremacy if investors continue to hold dominant economic power, no matter how progressive they may be. It's not wise to wait for investors to ask if profits are too high.

10

THE FIRST DUTY OF GOVERNMENT IS TO PROTECT WEALTH

The Myths of the Free Market and Takings

IN DEFINING DECOLONIZATION IN *The Wretched of the Earth*, Frantz Fanon summoned the biblical admonition, "The last shall be first." To decolonize is to put that sentence into practice, he said. It means starting not by asking the powerful to be more kind, but with the colonized claiming power: creating government by the people and for the people, "for the disinherited and by the disinherited," he wrote.[1]

The moment the political and economic power of European empire was nearing its zenith—when these empires would control 85 percent of the earth as colonies and possessions—was the moment when a wave of revolutions and war broke out, leaving five massive empires in the rubble. It began in 1908 when the Ottoman Empire fell to the revolutionary Young Turks. Soon a revolution toppled the Qing Dynasty of China, and the Russian Revolution crushed the rule of the Romanovs. After the guns of World War I fell silent in 1918, two more empires lay in ruins—that of the Hohenzollern, led by the swaggering Kaiser Wilhelm in Germany (who still claimed to rule by the long-discredited idea of divine right), and the Habsburg Empire in Austria-Hungary; it was that throne's presumptive heir, Franz Ferdinand, who'd been assassinated in the revolutionary move that lit the fuse of war.

In the United Kingdom, the façade of governance by the propertied elite endured, with the British throne still standing after World Wars I and II. Yet as Queen Elizabeth II occupied that throne an astonishing seventy years, she did so as a living fossil, watching her empire disintegrate while imperial possessions broke away to independence, as did the colonies of many other European powers. Gandhi had led India to break from the British Empire in 1947, followed by dozens of successful decolonizations in Africa and Asia in the 1950s, 1960s, and beyond, culminating in the downfall of white-settler apartheid in South Africa in 1994.

In the spirit of the times after WWI, Upton Sinclair titled his novel of the era *World's End*. A world was indeed ending. The settled, seemingly eternal, class-based governance regime of monarchy and aristocracy—which had endured for millennia as a predominant form of government across the globe—was crumbling.[2] A new paradigm of democracy was rising, as peoples in nation after nation demanded the right to self-determination they knew to be naturally theirs.

Yet as political regimes were democratizing—however chaotically, imperfectly, precariously—the property regimes of the world would take a different path.

With empire's demise, a struggle began to determine the principles that would govern the world economy. Would property regimes become democratic? Would the wealth of the capitalist/imperialist system be lost? Or would the elite privileges enjoyed under empire somehow continue in a new guise?

Shattered Empire: The Seedbed of Neoliberalism

The group that would settle the question came to be known as neoliberals. The story of their origin in the end of empire is told in a masterful analysis by Wellesley College historian Quinn Slobodian in his book *Globalists*.

Among neoliberalism's leading theorists was Austrian economist Ludwig von Mises, who believed an ideal society had nearly been realized before WWI—a rational world where captive nations of color supplied raw materials at low cost, while the wealthy elite of Europe owned the factories and banks that profited handsomely from manufacture. As he lamented in 1922, "Who then would rebuild the shattered world?"[3]

As war socialism had reared its head, Mises and fellow conservatives watched in horror as some foreign property was seized, command economies replaced supply and demand, and rationing replaced the price mechanism. "The space of the private capitalist was desecrated," Slobodian wrote.[4] The sacred nature of private property was violated. Industrialists and investors who'd thrived under the wing of empire felt themselves beset by threats all around.

German economist Wilhelm Röpke fretted about the "monstrous misuse of power" by farmers and labor unions, while Mises saw collective bargaining as the "gun under the table." Members of the organized working class were "barbarian invaders," capital controls an "act of aggression." Public demonstrations were described by Mises as tactics of "terror and intimidation." The years after 1945 saw the frightening innovation of universal human rights. Röpke spoke of the post-1945 spread of "rabies democratica."[5] The very idea of democracy entering into property relations was abhorrent to these men.

The democratic state, which neoliberals perceived as a "parasitical vine," had to be taken back from the masses. Their goal was to defang the state, to block its economic power, in the work of rebuilding the shattered utopia of global capitalism.[6]

As the neoliberals published and lectured over decades, gathering in the Mont Pelerin Society created by F. A. Hayek, Milton Friedman, and others in 1947, they pieced together a relatively coherent prescription for a new world order. As Slobodian observed, the neoliberalism they created was both an ideology and a project to restore class power. In concert with the International Chamber of Commerce, their aim was to defend the threatened privileges of wealth.[7]

To protect wealth supremacy.

A Doubled World

In place of the interwoven social order of monarchy and colonial possessions, the neoliberals envisioned a world no longer unitary but doubled: one world political, the other economic. One the world of government. The other the world of property.[8]

International investment had made it routine for people to own land, money, shares of stock, and enterprises scattered across the earth, in places investors had never set foot. Even military battles often left private property in place; after fighting ceased, that land or business (or diamond mine) was still yours. To safeguard the ownership of property and capital, the neoliberals believed respect for private property and investor rights needed to trump national law.[9]

There would be two worlds, yes, but one was to be superior, inviolable, and invisible—a borderless global world that economist Moritz Bonn termed "invisible economic empire."[10]

In the tradition of British theorist John Locke, the neoliberals saw the role of government as limited to providing security and protecting property rights, protecting the rights of wealth.[11]

Against human rights, they posed the *rights of capital*. Their borderless economic empire, Slobodian wrote, was one "in which the investor and the corporation—and not the citizen or refugee—was the paradigmatic rights-bearing subject." The rights of property and capital were sacrosanct. All others were seen as an interfering "special interest." Röpke floated the chilling—and eerily prescient—idea that to counteract mass democracy, it might become necessary to create authoritarian government. [12]

What neoliberals envisioned was a utopia for capital. They were patient in its pursuit, not confining themselves to the politically possible. As Swiss economist Michael Heilperin wrote in 1947, we must "seek goals which may appear unattainable ... until they have actually been reached."[13] For example, they wrote first drafts for international investment laws that seemed impossibly ideal for investors, yet ultimately became global norms. International investors gained power over national governments, using investor-state dispute-resolution mechanisms to sue and defeat laws that hindered profit taking.[14]

Over time, the neoliberals captured both public opinion and political power, as their ideas—once considered marginal and extreme—gained ascendancy with the era of Reagan and Thatcher. In system design terms, it was through the *infrastructure* of the International Monetary Fund and the World Trade Organization that neoliberal policies were imposed on much of the world. Most remarkably, neoliberalism was adopted even by parties once on the left, including Democrat and Labour leaders like Jimmy Carter, Bill Clinton, Tony Blair, and even, to a depressing extent, Barack Obama, who after the 2008 meltdown bailed out banks while leaving government and homeowners to shoulder the losses.

Today, we speak of neoliberal theory as the "free market," one of the modern myths essential to our property regime—taught in business schools, embraced by mainstream economists, and underlying the conservative policy agenda of limited government, deregulation, and low taxes.

THE MYTH OF THE FREE MARKET

Democracy is to be subdued, for it is the enemy of the independence and power of wealth. There shall be no limits on the field of action of corporations and capital. We call this a "free market."

The term *free market*—along with *free trade* and *free enterprise*—purports to show capitalism as the handmaiden of democracy, evoking that democratic value of freedom. In truth, the story of the birth of neoliberalism lays bare how the free market myth arose directly out of fear of democracy, as an effort to protect wealth from the policies a majority would choose.

Zombie Neoliberalism Walks

There has been much unmasking of the myth of the free market, with countless books showing how markets left to themselves do not self-regulate, as the neoliberal theory claims. It was the global financial crisis of 2008, followed by the global COVID-19 pandemic—both necessitating massive government action—that demonstrated the failing of this theory most recently.

After Bear Stearns and Lehman Brothers went down, threatening to pull the global financial system down with them, the Federal Reserve and Bank of England together used *quantitative easing* (QE)—bond and asset purchases that take debt off the hands of others, freeing up cash—to inject $3 trillion into the economy, in sums amounting to roughly 20 percent of GDP in both countries.[15]

With the COVID crisis and associated economic shutdowns, the world's four largest central banks stepped in with a still larger *$9 trillion* in QE.[16] On top of that came fiscal intervention, with Biden spending $1.9 trillion, including direct payments of up to $1,400 to individuals.[17] Soon after came $400 billion for climate and energy incentives.[18]

With the flick of a pen, governments had showed how our collective power was there to tackle financial collapse, climate change, pandemics, unemployment. Rather than some ideal picture of government so small it could be drowned in the bathtub—the erstwhile dream of lobbyist Grover Norquist (anybody remember him?)—government stood revealed as a colossus.

The neoliberal agenda of limited government, tax cuts, and deregulation seemed a zombie. Yet that undead agenda took up residence at 10 Downing Street, as new UK Prime Minister Liz Truss in 2022 announced she was enacting steep tax cuts for the wealthiest. Paired with new spending, this move was recognized as such lunacy that it sent financial markets into a tizzy and had to be walked back immediately. Soon Truss had become the shortest-serving British prime minister in history.[19]

Takings: The Terror of the Wealthy

To make sense of such lunacy, it's helpful to summon another myth of wealth supremacy—that of takings. Conservatives cling to their agenda of tax cuts and limited government because, as the parties of wealth, they're animated by wealth's greatest fear: that their wealth will be taken.

THE MYTH OF TAKINGS

The first duty of government is the protection of wealth. The US Constitution prohibits "takings" from the propertied elite, while that elite may take from others at will.

Protection against takings of property has a long pedigree in British law, which is the root law for global capitalism. This protection was asserted by barons on the field of Runnymede in 1215, as the king was forced to sign the Magna Carta, ensuring that land granted by the monarch became the permanent private property of the landed class, no longer subject to being retaken at the whim of the crown.

Property law, in its origin, is the law of the possession of land, which is considered "real property," or today, real estate. In agrarian society, land was the foundation on which the great estates of upper-class privilege stood. The law of land possession deeply shaped British society, infusing the British constitution to such an extent that the constitution at times seems, as Frederic William Maitland observed in his nineteenth-century *Constitutional History of England*, "but an appendix to the law of real property."[20]

Protection of property was vital to the founders of the United States as well. It was a concern they threaded through the US Constitution, as they sought to protect private property—including their own landed estates, their slaves and plantations—from takings by a politically empowered yet economically dispossessed majority. "The first object of government," wrote James Madison in Federalist #10, is protection of the "diversity in the faculties of men, from which the rights of property originate."[21] In short, the first object of government is protection of property.

Most egregiously, the Constitution protected property in slaves, prohibiting Congress from outlawing the Atlantic slave trade for twenty years; adding a fugitive slave clause requiring the return of runaway slaves; and empowering slave states through the chilling clause counting the enslaved as three-fifths of a person in political representation.

Beyond slavery, protection of property was enshrined in the principle that only property owners could vote—a principle broadly embraced at the time, though not written into the federal Constitution because voting qualifications were delegated to the states. When the Constitution was written, for example, New York State limited voting to those with an estate of one hundred pounds. That meant that in 1790, only twelve hundred people out of a New York City population of thirty thousand possessed the wealth to vote. A landed aristocracy controlled elections.[22]

There were also the takings clauses of the Fifth and Fourteenth Amendments, stipulating that private property shall not be taken for public use without just compensation or due process of law.

Deeply consequential for our own day was the design of the Senate and Electoral College, which insulated against direct majority rule and protected the disproportionate power of slaveholding states.[23] This was a conscious protection of wealth. During debates on the Constitution, Madison argued the Senate should be constituted so as to "protect the minority of the opulent against the majority."[24]

Taking: The Essential Action of Capitalism

Certainly it's vital to protect private property. No one who owns a house or land or a business would like to see it taken. There is wisdom in how the founders protected property, as in much that they did.

But their view of taking is incomplete until we observe how they were blind to their own takings from others. The estates they jealously guarded stood on land taken from Native Americans. The African slaves they recognized as property were brutally taken from their homelands, their very bodies taken from their own control.

The fear of takings by the wealthy tends to be a one-way fear. It fails to acknowledge how wealth often comes through taking from others. The British lord of the manor had always taken from the peasants. Brothers and husbands took the property of sisters and wives, who could own nothing. In the predatory mortgages leading up to 2008, abusive mortgage lenders took the home equity from Black homeowners, the property rights of Black people somehow seeming not to weigh in the balance of forces.

Taking is a matter of perspective. It's a matter of bias. And too often, taking is the essential action of our capital-centric property regime.

We see this in private equity buying up rental properties and raising rents. Corporations taking from workers the increases in productivity their labor creates. Hedge funds operating dirty fossil fuel assets, taking from the biosphere its ability to sustain life.

From the perspective of capital, all of this isn't taking. It's "wealth creation."

Regulation of business, now that's a taking—taking the ability to maximize profits. Government taxes are a taking. The neoliberal agenda of limited government, low taxes, and deregulation is all about avoiding takings by government.

Yet it's about something else as well. Something bigger—something implicit yet left unstated by neoliberal theory: *a mandate to government to keep hands off and let the machine of capital extraction run unimpeded.*

In essence, the free-market concept is a fig leaf. It's an ideological shield, designed to protect the real action, which lies deeper, in the power of wealth, free and safe in its own invisible empire, where it remains infinitely hungry for more. Neoliberalism is the cheerleader of the machine of extraction. Wealth extraction is the real game.

11

EXTRACTION
IN THE EXTREME

How Financialization Drives Today's Crises

THE MACHINE OF CAPITAL EXTRACTION has been left quite
free to run unimpeded since the 1980s, thanks to the long dominance
of neoliberalism in policy. The result has been financialization—that
state of affairs in which the financial economy is eating the real economy, as we began to explore in chapter 7.

Most prominent among the beneficiaries are the wealthiest 1 percent of the world's population, who now own about 46 percent—nearly
half—of all the world's wealth, according to Credit Suisse.[1] A tiny handful of people—just ten individuals (not even enough to make up a full
soccer team)—own an astronomical $1.5 trillion in combined wealth.[2]

The more wealth is diverted away from the real economy and into
the financial world, the richer these plutocrats become. Since 1980,
the top 1 percent has been grabbing about *three times* as much income
as has the bottom half of the population.[3]

We lack the standard conceptual frames to help us grasp what's
really going on here. The significant activity in the system now falls
outside customary measures like GDP. Even Thomas Piketty's widely
heralded *Capital in the Twenty-First Century*, cited in chapter 7,
focused only on the capital income that shows up in GDP. But GDP

is an inadequate measure for a financialized economy. Since 1980, the truly staggering upward leaps of wealth have come from elsewhere—from capital gains that remain "unrealized" (not cashed out): the gains in the asset prices of real estate, stocks, and bonds.

Figure 11.1 shows the startling growth of total asset values (including both income and unrealized gains), based on analysis by economists Michael Hudson, Dirk Bezemer, and Howard Reed in their study of the US economy.

The paper's authors show this has come about because we're not using our wealth productively but extractively. We still discuss capitalism as a system of production and consumption, and this may be how the system is justified, but it's no longer how it functions. The system now *drains income flows* from production and consumption to support higher asset valuations.[4]

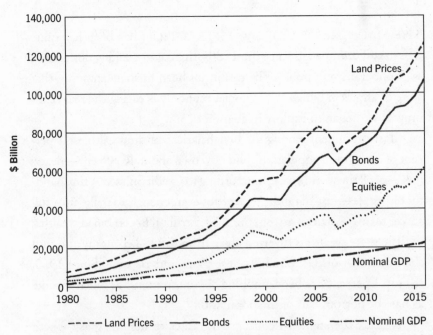

Source: Chart based on data from Howard Reed, Landman Economics. Analysis from Michael Hudson and Dirk Bezemer, "Rent-Seeking and Asset Price Inflation: A Total Returns Profile of Economic Polarization in America," *Review of Keynesian Economics* 9, no. 4 (October 2021).

FIGURE 11.1: Meteoric growth of US asset wealth vs. GDP growth

In a dialogue with my colleagues and I at the Democracy Collaborative, the authors spoke with us in language far more blunt than their academic paper, with Dirk putting it this way: "Much of the financial sector is parasitic. It's not creating value but skimming off value."[5]

A swelling of debt is one way this is accomplished. For example, when private equity buys firms, it often places substantial new debt on those portfolio companies, then uses the cash to write the PE fund and its investors a large check, in a sleight-of-hand maneuver benignly named *dividend recapitalization*. Once the PE fund sells that firm, the company is left responsible for paying down the onerous debt, which often means cutting staffing levels in order to manage the cash outflow. Income to labor has been drained. Income to finance has been boosted. And in a significant number of instances, debt-laden firms end up bankrupt.

We see the same redirection of flows inside publicly traded corporations. Major corporations in recent years have pretty much stopped investing their profits in research and innovation or in paying higher wages, instead directing the lion's share of profits to share buybacks and dividends paid out to shareholders. A study in the *Harvard Business Review*—bluntly titled "Why Stock Buybacks Are Dangerous for the Economy"—showed that between 2009 and 2018, companies in the S&P 500 used an astronomical *91 percent of net income* on these two forms of payouts to shareholders. Much of what the firms invested in turned out to be thin air: inflated stock market valuations that later deflated. (Though often not before CEOs profited handsomely.)[6]

According to Gerald Epstein and Juan Antonio Montecino at the University of Massachusetts Amherst, if all this sucking action by finance weren't going on—if the financial sector had remained its optimal size, performing its traditional, useful roles—the typical US household would have enjoyed *double* the wealth at retirement.[7]

As the "Too Much Finance" economists at the IMF have showed, finance contributes to a country's development only up to a certain point. Beyond that size, it starts to *reduce* economic growth and inflict many kinds of damage.

Nicholas Shaxson, a financial journalist who writes for the *Financial Times*, the *Economist*, and elsewhere, calls this perverse process "the finance curse" in his book of the same name. "All this wealth is a sign of sickness, not health," he writes.

The societal-level result is that our economy of, by, and for wealth is increasingly brittle today. As this system reaches its swollen, financialized peak, its ongoing processes of wealth extraction are driving or profiting from many of the large crises of our time.

Tallying the Staggering Costs of Financialization

First among the painful costs is inequality, or what we might better call *asset poverty*. I'm referring here to the anxious existence of those *two out of three* Americans with nothing to fall back on in an emergency, who can't cover an unexpected expense of even $1,000.[8] The FIRE sector is creating this inequality. When corporations restructure for profit growth, that creates massive unemployment. That in turn reduces consumer spending, stifling economic growth. At the same time, concentrated wealth in the hands of the few enables them to bid up real estate prices beyond the reach of ordinary families.

There's the hollowing out of Main Street businesses and family firms. When private equity buys up firms and repackages them into conglomerates, that contributes to industry concentration and monopoly power. It inhibits the growth of small and medium-size enterprises and startups, which are the primary source of jobs and once offered reliable paths to stable middle-class lives. When investors and venture capital are interested only in "unicorns" with mammoth returns, regular businesses are starved of the investments that might offer steady, reasonable returns.

There's the executive wealth from stock options that keeps firms like Exxon pumping oil and willfully creating the climate of confusion that for so long blocked public clarity. And there are deeper, more subtle forces of wealth contributing to our broader inability to tackle climate change, with the uber-wealthy fueling hard-right think tanks that hobble the will of the majority.

Then there's the risk of financial instability. Corporate debt buildup and stock market bubbles create instability as corporations default and bubbles deflate. Under neoliberalism, that in turn means bailouts that shift the burden onto workers, communities, and taxpayers.[9]

The New Imperative: Eradicate Democracy

That brings us to the final risk of financialization: risk to democracy.

With the world facing unprecedented crises and forms of collapse, with politically energized young people having voted en masse for socialists like Bernie Sanders and Jeremy Corbyn, with dispossessed people of color on the verge of coalescing into new democratic majorities, with climate change threatening the growth imperative built into capitalism—and with all of this occurring even as the shield of neoliberalism has begun to fray at the edges—new approaches to wealth protection desperately needed to be found.[10]

The old neoliberal Röpke was right. To protect the wealth machine, it had become necessary to create authoritarian government. It had become necessary to eradicate *rabies democratica*.

12

A SOCIETY
HALF PLUTOCRATIC,
HALF DEMOCRATIC

The Crisis of Democracy

AS TRUMP SENT HIS minions to storm the US Capitol on January 6, 2021—a day that will live in infamy—my wife and I and millions watched it live on TV, as the chanting horde descended on the building, broke down barricades, penetrated hapless police lines, smashed through locked doors, and took over congressional chambers, leaving House Speaker Nancy Pelosi and Vice President Mike Pence to flee for their lives.

The blow inflicted on democracy has spread like an infected wound. Trump's Big Lie of a stolen election—believed at one point by an alarming 70 percent of Republicans—has metastasized into a cancer on democracy.[1] In the 2022 midterm US election, doubt was cast on Biden's victory by more than *370 Republican candidates*, the vast majority of Republicans running for the US House and Senate and top state offices.[2]

Many of these candidates failed to win election. Yet the infection is now growing systemically, through a malignant movement for voter suppression. As *Dark Money* author Jane Mayer wrote, a well-funded, national movement has used the Big Lie to advance changes in how ballots are cast and counted in forty-nine states, passing state laws, stripping the powers of election officials, aiming to place "antifraud" players in key offices.[3]

Chad Campbell, formerly Democratic minority leader in the Arizona House of Representatives, told Mayer the state was facing a "nonviolent overthrow." He said it's subtle because it's not happening with weapons. "But it's still a complete overthrow of democracy. They're trying to disenfranchise everyone who is not older white guys."[4]

"Epistemic warfare" is how Jonathan Rauch of the Brookings Institution explained it to the *Economist*.[5]

The Unseen Ruling Class

Behind it all—the cancerous cells threatening the body politic—lies the dark money of plutocratic conservative wealth. Dark money is working to make undermining democracy the new aim of the party of wealth. Mayer pointed out how the Koch network, sponsored by just four hundred of the wealthiest people in the country, had in 2016 created a political network—a permanent, private political machine—with a payroll larger than the entire Republican National Committee.[6] These are the players ready to stop at nothing to keep the machine of financial extraction going.

Billionaire funders, think tanks, groups like the corporate-funded American Legislative Exchange Council, which writes model state laws—this broad conservative movement has evolved to become an aggressive, coordinated assault on democracy. "It's a massive covert operation run by a small group of billionaire elites," Democratic senator Sheldon Whitehouse told Mayer. These powerful interests, with virtually unlimited money, have moved on from other priorities. Their focus now, he said, is "manipulating that most precious of American gifts—the vote."[7]

Deeply woven into this effort are racial fears and resentments. One pundit told Mayer the Big Lie didn't require proof, because it was animated by the belief that Biden won because of voters who aren't real Americans. Black and brown voters. Immigrants. Nonwhites of all kinds.

The white supremacy at work is closely intertwined with wealth supremacy. As W. E. B. Du Bois explained nearly a century ago, white elites avoid economic redistribution and cling to power by offering marginalized whites "a public and psychological wage"—a way to feel superior to more marginalized people of color. Whites may be poor, unemployed, or precariously employed, yet they're the real Americans.[8]

If this role of race in the antidemocracy agitation has been widely discussed, often overlooked is the role of plutocrats, as political scientists Jacob Hacker and Paul Pierson have observed. In their book *Let Them Eat Tweets*, they emphasized that Trump's rise can be understood only in the context of the decades-long shift in the political environment that preceded him. "That shift is the rise of plutocracy—government of, by, and for the rich," they wrote.[9] Republicans escalated white backlash in order to advance a plutocratic agenda otherwise unlikely to garner popular support.

What remade American politics was runaway inequality—that offspring of financialization, which created the expanding pool of disaffected, destabilized whites hungry for their psychological wage, while also creating the wealth that shifted policy toward corporations and the rich.

Also at work was contempt for government. For decades, the Koch brothers and neoliberals vilified the very concept of government, laying the groundwork for the literal attacks on policy makers of our day. As Mayer noted, whatever dislike for Trump the Kochs held, he was their "natural heir." Trump's proposals—eliminating the estate tax, for example—were steps toward installing a permanent aristocracy in America.[10]

The rise of plutocracy is the story of post-1980 politics, Hacker and Pierson wrote. Senator Whitehouse agreed. He wrote of how corporate and wealth influence in elections had "exploded" in recent decades, as campaign finance became "virtually lawless." "Never in my life have I seen such a complex web of front groups sowing deliberate deceit to create public confusion about issues that should be clear," he wrote in his book *Captured*. As the dark money behind these front groups added to the long-time influence of corporations over Washington, Whitehouse said, what arose was an "unseen ruling class."[11]

The rise of that ruling class paralleled in precise ways the rise of financialized wealth, both exploding around 1980: that Reagan–Thatcher moment when the machine of capital extraction was set loose.

We Cannot Sustain the Unsustainable

Even on its own terms, the machine of wealth extraction is becoming unsustainable. The European Systemic Risk Board has issued a rare "general warning" about the increasing probability of "tail-risk scenarios"—low-likelihood catastrophes. It warned of how risks to financial stability may materialize simultaneously, amplifying each other's impact.[12]

Kristalina Georgieva, the International Monetary Fund's managing director, has said the world is moving from a period of "relative predictability," with low interest rates and low inflation, into an era of heightened economic fragility. Ahead, she said, lies "greater uncertainty, higher economic volatility, geopolitical confrontations, and more frequent and devastating natural disasters."[13]

Yet even as the system gyrates, with asset prices increasingly unstable, we keep hoping to prop the system up. Michael Hudson notes that quantitative easing—those trillions pumped into the economy by central banks, as discussed in chapter 10—supported the prices of assets, rather than permitting asset prices to fall and wipe out some of the claims by the wealthy against the rest of us.

This attempt to sustain the unsustainable is unlikely to succeed in the long run, Hudson argues. Debts that cannot be paid simply won't be.[14]

Still, the capital-centric system's magical thinking lulls us into believing asset prices will climb forever, lulls us into hoping they will. The S&P 500 index between 2009 and 2021 grew to seven times its size.[15] *Seven times.* Yet in the way we think about investing, the way portfolios are managed, we act as though the S&P at some point will simply resume its climb—as though pure numbers can mount upward forever, detached from a reality where our world lurches from one crisis to another, where Pakistan found itself one-third underwater, where *two out of three* Americans are one small emergency away from disaster.

To imagine we can make this system a little less bad is to practice appeasement, while the other side is engaged in all-out war.

A world half plutocratic and half democratic cannot long endure. One half will eventually supersede the other. This is occurring today before our eyes, as the plutocratic economy attempts to consume the democratic polity. The alternative, the solution commensurate with the problem, is system change—suffusing democracy into our economy, and building the new political-economic system now necessary to our survival.[16]

PART III

WHERE WE BEGIN

MY PERSONAL AWAKENING FROM the trance of our system's myths has taken decades. My journey began in the late 1980s as I cofounded *Business Ethics*, joining the tiny band of progressives reimagining business and investing, stepping with them into the citadel of power that feels forbidden to most of us, claiming power long taboo for me personally—my father hadn't allowed me to work in our small family business, as he had my brothers.

As I was launching my company, I dreamed one night of entering a church, a bank, in dream logic both, where male banker-priests stood murmuring among themselves behind an altar rail. That barrier marked the consecrated area where the congregation could not enter, where it was unthinkable I would have served as an altar girl, where no woman dared stand as a priest. In my dream, I stepped into that sanctuary. I knew, suddenly, that I belonged. I began to picture how to remodel the space, widen it, welcome others in. Claim it as our own. Because we all belong.

In the more than three decades since, I've written about, helped design, and participated in more promising experiments, models, and pathways for a democratic, regenerative, antiracist economy than I can count. The models and approaches we need are here.

Yet instead of the democratic economy so many have worked to build, we now have a financialized economy. A system that remains largely on autopilot. The track it runs on is made up of all the norms we accept as necessary, technical, commonplace.

As I noted in the introduction to part II, the track it runs on, in short, is mindset. Our mindset.

We participate in system change when we change our minds. When we wake up to see that things can be different.

It begins with naming, as we saw in part I—naming wealth supremacy, seeing how pervasive the unjust norms of capital bias are, how contrary they are to the ideals of democratic society. That's the first step in our theory of system change.

From naming we moved in part II to the second step in our theory: challenging the legitimacy of the system, unmasking the myths that obscure how the system is rigged against us, revealing those myths as absurd. When such illusions are exposed to the light of day, it is the beginning of the end of the old paradigm.

In part II we explored another essential aspect of system change: necessity—recognizing the raw need to move beyond the current system, as we come to grips with the brutal, wide-reaching damages wrought by financialization, irrefutably documented by economists.

Now, in part III, we cover the final steps in our theory of system change: imagination, demonstration, and pathways.

Imagination   We possess a massive power—the power to imagine that an entire next system is possible. As we ourselves change our minds, we can help others awaken through pranks and subversive acts, as well as through calling for powerful new metrics that help our society see what is actually going on.

Demonstration   Demonstrating viable alternative models— like the entire state of Nebraska being powered by cooperative and municipal energy; or the cooperative banks in Germany, the Sparkasse, which control 30 percent of bank assets yet do 70 percent of lending to small- and medium-size enterprises—proves that other ways are economically practical as well as transformational.

Pathways   The final step in our theory of system change is designing the many pathways by which we get from here to there, by which we limit the power of the extractive paradigm and spread the models and approaches of the democratic economy. This includes using crises as opportunities, advancing solutions that not only solve crises but build system change at the same time. And it includes starting where we live, in our communities, where growing numbers of cities, regions, and even entire nations like Scotland are building the democratic economy through the economic development practices known as community wealth building.

Some of the pathways explored here are substantial and well developed, others are new and small. I find myself thinking back to the days when solar power was a countercultural idea that showed up in the Whole Earth Catalog, a fringe concept that seemed unlikely ever to produce 115 billion kilowatt-hours, as it did in 2021.[1]

Improbable change happens all the time. The extractive system is not inevitable and eternal. We can break its spell.

13

BREAKING THE TRANCE

*We Participate in System Change
When We Change Our Minds*

PATAGONIA FOUNDER YVON CHOUINARD startled the world when he announced his decision to donate the $3 billion of value in his company to a trust and nonprofit organization, which would use profits and resources to tackle climate change. People were puzzled, inspired, astonished.[1]

He's not alone. After his announcement I spoke with my friend Kate Emery, founder of a fifty-person IT and digital marketing consulting company, Walker Group, who had sought my guidance in transferring her ownership into a perpetual trust, not as a gift but as a sale on reasonable, mildly concessionary terms. I've worked with and encountered many business leaders like Kate and Yvon. Even more numerous are the investors eager to play a role in building a more fair, more democratic economy.

One example is the opportunity my wife and I recently jumped on when our investment advisor shared it—to make a loan to Oweesta, a Native American CDFI, at barely above zero returns, to further its vital work of development in Indian country. When our advisor offered this opportunity to all their clients, they found many takers. The investment firm gave up its own management fees on those investments.

The strongest power on earth, in the longer run, may not be extractive capital, that rickety set of overblown claims by a tiny elite that must relentlessly grow or collapse. Life, the planet—that's the ultimate force, the force that flows through us, that is us, including our minds, our hearts, the force of us when we think together and act together to protect what we cherish.

"Gaia is a system of wisdom, sharing, caring," Kate said to me. "It's much more egalitarian, it's a community." It's a system much like democracy. Like the kind of system Kate installed at her company, which for years has shared profits equally among the community, the workers, and the shareholders. As she retires and steps back, the new trust ownership design will preserve that approach, safeguarding in perpetuity the firm's purpose of making the world a better place, even as it continues its traditional consulting work.

Kate told me she had a hard time finding an attorney to carry out the new ownership design she wanted, which was to be accompanied by a new governance design where select employee stewards would ensure the firm's purpose was carried out. Lawyers pushed her to sell "the thing" for the highest price, then use the proceeds for philanthropy. But she persisted. She recognized her company isn't an object but a living system, with a purpose of serving life, and she's using enterprise design—the system design elements of ownership, governance, purpose—to ensure that what she has built will endure. She's putting in place a piece of the democratic economy. And she may write a book to show others how to do what she's done.

Kate didn't speak of Gaia to her attorneys. People think it's too soft and dreamy, not hard-nosed like business, this successful businesswoman said to me. "I mean, what a fantasy capitalism is," she added with a laugh. "Someday we'll look back on capitalism and say, wow, wasn't that a crazy idea?"

What Kate is doing with her business, what Yvon did with Patagonia, what Oweesta investors and Oweesta itself are doing, what the investment firm did in giving up fees on those investments—these are all subversive acts. They're all declarations, in their own ways, that maximizing is no longer our religion. There are things we care more about.

Can such acts make a difference? Yes. In fact, they're vital—sending out ripples beyond themselves. These acts are helping to break the trance of the normality of the system-as-is. Helping us all to wake up. They're the kind of change of mind where system change begins.

Out of all the ways we try to change capitalism—laws, regulatory agencies, counting and measuring different outcomes, creating new institutions—systems theorist Donella Meadows reminded us that the single most effective place to intervene in any system is at *the level of mindset*: the mind out of which the system arises. The paradigm. What constitutes a paradigm, she wrote, is society's deepest set of beliefs about how the world works, the shared idea in our minds: "the great big unstated assumptions—unstated because unnecessary to state; everyone already knows them."[2]

No One to Shoot

Recall those scenes in John Steinbeck's novel *The Grapes of Wrath* where farmers being forced off their land in the Dust Bowl start packing guns. When a foreclosure agent tells them to leave, they ask, Who's to blame? Who can they shoot? "It ain't nobody. It's a company," they're told. One farmer blows out the headlights of a tractor with a shotgun.[3] But there isn't anyone to shoot. If they took out an agent, a few bankers, others would take their place. Corporations sell dirty assets, private equity buys them. Unions gain power, employment is disaggregated into Uberized bits. The various regulations and interventions we try, the system flows around them.

Where the soul of the regime lives is in *the idea of the regime*. What's in control is *the paradigm* of wealth extraction.

Paradigms may seem harder to change than anything else, Meadows wrote. "But there's nothing physical or expensive or even slow in the process of paradigm change," she continued. "In a single individual it can happen in a millisecond. All it takes is a click in the mind, a falling of scales from eyes, a new way of seeing."[4]

The place to begin to transform the extractive economy is at the level of our own mind. This is where we stop participating. This is where the system begins to lose its grip. This is where we begin to win.

Capitalism Is Nothing without Our Cooperation

The acts of people like Yvon Chouinard, Kate Emery, and the investors in Oweesta are all acts of hope, cracks in the armor of fear and despair that encases so many of us. They're a way to begin breaking the grip of what author Mark Fisher calls "capitalist realism": the belief that capitalism is the only system possible, that any other system is not even imaginable, so don't bother.

Fisher opened his book *Capitalist Realism* with the quotation, "It's easier to imagine the end of the world than the end of capitalism." That's a sense that pervades our culture like a dense fog, part of the ethos that leaves the extractive system to its untroubled functioning—"metabolizing and absorbing anything with which it comes into contact," Fisher wrote.[5]

The "realism" at work, he said, "is analogous to the deflationary perspective of a depressive," who sees hope as a dangerous illusion. This depression is fed in us by the "massive desacralization of culture" that capitalism involves, the loss of shared belief in moral meaning, leaving us with a culture where only money and wealth matter. This is presumed to be true for virtually everyone, and only fools believe otherwise. Lawyers pressured Kate to sell her firm to the highest bidder. Most founders do.

We believe we're doing what we have to do. Yet this impotence "is not a passive observation of an already existing state of affairs," Fisher wrote. "It is a self-fulfilling prophecy."[6]

He added two insights: First, that capitalism is a "hyper-abstract impersonal structure" (an idea, an abstraction, not located only in particular individuals, as with, say, evil or narcissism). Second, that because of its abstract impersonality, capitalism *would be nothing without our cooperation* [emphasis added].[7]

These truths are hard to grasp. We point the finger at billionaires, CEOs, the 1 percent, hedge fund managers. It's harder to get the deeper truth Fisher pointed to—that "the centerlessness of global capitalism is radically unthinkable," that there are no overall controllers. This is something, he wrote, we find impossible to accept.[8]

When we stop seeing this system as inevitable, we step outside its centerless mind. And we begin to create—in our minds and hearts, in our culture, over time in institutions—the moral fundamentals of a next system.

14

PRANKS, NEW NAMING, AND OTHER SUBVERSIVE ACTS

Helping Others to Awaken

"HERE'S MY PLAN to save Twitter: let's buy it." That was the headline of the op-ed Nathan Schneider published in the *Guardian* on September 29, 2016, which launched a wide-reaching and still ongoing activist campaign. Schneider is an assistant professor at the University of Colorado Boulder, and a long-time advocate of cooperative ownership. His article spread across Twitter, with hundreds retweeting it, some adding #WeAreTwitter. The idea was to convert Twitter into a cooperative, owned and controlled by its users, as all cooperatives are.[1]

It was a prank, a thought experiment, a gesture meant to wake people up and advance the movement for a democratic economy. But it was also an idea that struck people as sensible. As an article in *Wired* said, "It makes perfect sense." Twitter, after all, is a kind of public utility. It's a public square, relied upon by journalists, policy makers, activists, and countless others—one of the handful of digital platforms we all rely on for so much of our lives. Yet we have no meaningful control. What if we owned and controlled Twitter?[2]

The suggestion sparked attention in large part because we have such a limited imagination about ownership. In Silicon Valley, companies aspire either to go public or to be acquired by a large competitor, both of which feed firms into the grip of big capital.

The campaign launched by the op-ed urged Twitter not to "sell its users to Wall Street." That campaign became a petition with thousands of signatures. And the petition evolved into a shareholder proposal the group sought to place on the company's "proxy ballot," the annual mechanism by which shareholders select directors and vote on other matters. Advanced with the help of longtime shareholder activist Jim McRitchie of CorpGov.net, the proposal asked the company to study its options for users to buy Twitter through a cooperative or a similar structure with broad-based ownership and accountability.

Twitter appealed to the Securities and Exchange Commission (SEC) to allow it to exclude the proposal from its ballot, on grounds that it interfered in day-to-day management. But "the SEC offered us an opportunity to appeal," Danny Spitzberg, one of the campaign's leaders, told me; his day job is lead researcher at Turning Basin Labs, a California-based staffing cooperative. The SEC wanted the group to file counterarguments to Twitter's opposition, emphasizing the importance of exploring ownership alternatives. The group did file. And the SEC sided with them, directing Twitter to put the proposal to a vote.[3]

It lost, as do most such activist resolutions. Yet the effort raised a ruckus, stirred valuable conversations, and enjoyed coverage in places like *Vanity Fair* and the *Financial Times*, which called the idea "a dream worthy of consideration." Even Albert Wenger of Union Square Ventures, one of Twitter's early major investors, wrote a blog supporting #BuyTwitter, saying experimentation with ownership models was essential to avoid social media platforms extracting too much from users and thus damaging the user loyalty that made them valuable.[4]

In the years following that 2017 shareholder meeting, after Twitter had been purchased by Elon Musk, the campaign stirred to life again in a new form: the formation of a Twitter Users' Assembly. Launched in January 2023, the assembly is drawing together a diversity of Twitter users—in particular, people working in journalism, whose professional and ethical duties make it easy to reimagine Twitter as a public news utility serving the public good. The users' assembly will develop proposals on how to make a platform like Twitter serve the public interest (BetterPlatform.net/).[5]

Spitzberg and Schneider are among the leading activists working for a democratic economy movement. That phrase, "democratic economy movement," might properly belong in quotation marks because, in truth, there isn't much of a movement. Mostly there are siloed communities pursuing isolated activities, lacking unified language or unity of purpose.

The cooperative world did get behind the Twitter campaign, with fifty leading organizations—from the National Cooperative Business Association to credit unions and law firms—signing a letter to Twitter shareholders supporting the proposal. Yet more typically, Spitzberg said to me, "The cooperative world is a little self-centered. The usual cast of characters get together at conferences," mostly talking to each other. "This is not going to shift who has wealth," he said emphatically. The Twitter campaign, by contrast, involved many kinds of people, far beyond the usual folks; it was the kind of movement prank that challenges power, helping to delegitimize the idea that Twitter exists solely to extract maximum wealth from it, spreading the idea that the platform should naturally serve the public interest. It's an example of how you start to build a movement.

Acting Up to Wake Us Up

We need more pranks like this. By "prank," I mean some deliberate act designed to draw attention—sometimes with humor, sometimes with shock—and make us see the unspoken biases we live with, like the crazy idea that one wealthy man should own and control the public square. Pranks are a way of subverting the sober rules of the system. While they're fun, they're also deadly serious.

In our theory of system change, pranks, renaming, and subversive acts are part of the delegitimizing efforts that can undermine the current system and empower a movement. Renaming helps us to see the water in which we swim. This is what feminists did in the 1970s with the invention of Ms., a neutral alternative to the traditional Mrs. and Miss, which identify women by their relationship to men. It's happening in the abortion debate, with new terms like *reproductive freedom*, *reproductive justice*, and *forced pregnancy*—all of which reposition the dialogue in powerful ways.

This kind of renaming leads naturally to recognizing bias, to seeing its illegitimacy. When we name and call out bias, it's also a way of coming together, building power. A potent example is the #MeToo movement, which began as a social media hashtag and built into a massive movement that created real-world changes: CEOs ousted, candidates brought down, public figures disgraced. #MeToo today calls itself a "league of disruptors." As its website says, it's "More Than a Viral Hashtag; It's a Movement for Justice and Healing for Sexual Violence Survivors" (*MeTooMvmt.org/*).

What if the democratic economy movement began renaming in more deliberate ways? We've seen a few examples of that in past chapters. Bill Baue of r3.0 initiative is delegitimizing the traditional notion of materiality with his open letter critiquing the framework of the International Sustainability Standards Board and calling its approach to sustainability "Sociopathic Materiality."[6] That's a great bit of prankish renaming.

The concept of "intergenerational fiduciary duty" explored in chapter 6 is another example of great renaming, one with deeper roots in intellectual analysis.

When we name and measure things differently, we can begin to see our economy differently. Here are some ideas.

Productive vs. Speculative Investment

We should begin to distinguish *productive investment* from *speculative investment*. "This distinction does not exist in the financial discourse today," said economist Dirk Bezemer. Long discussed by theorists of capitalism, it's a distinction so fundamental that it might be likened to that between *renewable* and *nonrenewable resources*, first articulated by E. F. Schumacher in *Small Is Beautiful*, which has had an incalculable impact on ecological thought.[7]

Imagine a world where investor portfolios are required to designate investments as *productive* or *speculative*. These investments could be treated differently in, for example, taxes or corporate voting rights. Such naming could potentially shift more and more investments toward productive use in the real world. As Bezemer put it, "We cannot change reality until we name reality."[8]

How we currently name investments can cloak their true nature. We say we "invest" in companies on public markets, but in the vast majority of cases, we're not providing productive capital to those firms. We're speculators, buying shares in the hope their value will rise. Money touches down inside a company only when it issues new shares, with an initial public offering or subsequent secondary offerings. For most companies, such offerings are relatively rare—a topic I explored at length in *The Divine Right of Capital*.[9]

Textbooks speak of shareholders providing capital "inputs" into corporations, but there's precious little inputting going on in public stock markets. One way to highlight this is for researchers, possibly MBA students, to document the true nature of shareholder inputs in one corporation.

As a thought experiment, let's say that fifty years ago Acme Company (producer of giant anvils, slingshots, and dynamite sticks) floated an initial public offering to fund the machinery, labor, and raw materials for production. Those shares were sold at $10. A half century later, shares trade at $300. Dividends per share over fifty years total another, say, $250. Original shares have now garnered returns of $550 for a productive input of $10—a return of 55 to 1.

Still, Acme continues to bend over backward to keep share price high—even though it's long past the time it got the productive funding needed to make the world scarier for coyotes and keep its ineffectual products on the market (Wile E. Coyote lives).

At what point have the original shareholders received enough? Why is this obligation eternal? At what point does continued shareholder extraction become unjust enrichment? Who decides? The answer is, it's up to us, the body politic, to challenge and evolve the rules that produced a system so unfit for the daunting challenges of the twenty-first century.

Workers as Members of the Corporation

Here's another idea: a prank to challenge the fiction that workers are not members of the corporation. Workers could run candidates for board seats at their place of employment. They could hold parallel elections, with worker-selected nominees. When these worker directors are refused formal acceptance as board members, as they no doubt would be, start a conversation: Why aren't workers members of the corporation? Who made that decision and how well is it working out? How does muting workers' voices serve any goal beyond profit maximization?

More tangibly, when a company division is sold off, workers could buy that division and own it through an employee stock ownership plan (ESOP). This kind of move is well known in ESOP circles; it's done with bank debt, and ESOP experts are out there who can help.[10]

Measuring the Precariat

Part-time, temporary, self-employed, contract, and gig work have spread in massive ways that we don't clearly see, because we have no official statistics tracking this phenomenon. As we saw in chapter 8, the GAO pegged it at 40 percent of the labor force in 2015, but hasn't published similar figures since.

The GAO's report called it the "contingent workforce."[11] A better name is the *precariat*, a term circulating in the public discourse. If we named and documented the precariat workforce through a precariat metric, it could spark discussion in the press: Why is precarity so high? What forces are behind this?

Financial-Sector GDP vs. Real-Sector GDP

The figure of GDP is almost quaint in today's financialized economy. It's like using a rotary phone in the era of the cell phone. New kinds of national reporting are needed.

Bezemer suggests we decompose GDP into two parts: the growth of the financial sector (*financial-sector GDP*) and the growth of the rest of the economy (*real-sector GDP*), which is the real economy of jobs and spending on goods and services. When we separate these two, we see that about one-third of GDP is being extracted out by finance. And that extraction is vastly larger than in the past.

Between 1970 and 2019 in the UK, financial-sector GDP rose from 13 percent to 33 percent of GDP (see figure 14.1).[12]

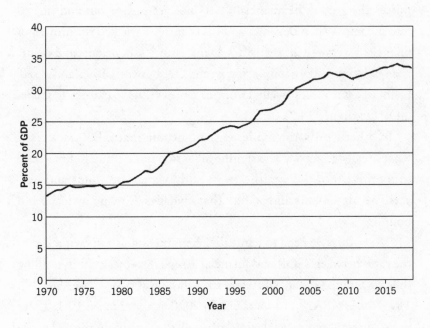

Source: Organization for Economic Cooperation and Development, https://stats.oecd.org/ Index.aspx? DataSetCode=STANI4_2020. Calculations by Dirk Bezemer, Michael Hudson, and Howard Reed, "Exploring the Capital Gains Economy: The Case of the UK," 2022 unpublished working paper commissioned by the Democracy Collaborative.

FIGURE 14.1: Finance, insurance, and real estate (FIRE) sector as a proportion of Gross Value Added, a measure of GDP, UK, 1970–2019

In other words, we as a society are now paying the folks who move around money—managing investments, running hedge funds—fully one-third of all the income in our economy. That means that for the vast majority of people, the growing income in the economy never reaches them. It's siphoned off by financial professionals and their organizations. But this is obscured in conventional national accounting.

The Unified Financial Assets to Income Ratio: The UNFAIR Metric

There's a second way that GDP fails to show us what's going on in the financialized economy: GDP only tracks income. It misses wealth. It misses the growth of financial assets not yet cashed out and turned into income. When Bezemer and his coauthors tracked the growth of financial assets—debt securities, loans, equities, pensions, and insurance holdings—they found that in the UK between 1995 and 2020, financial asset values swelled from six times GDP to close to *ten times* GDP (see figure 14.2).

In other words, the modest rise in income that GDP tracks isn't what's really going on. The significant action has shifted to finance—to the wealth of the wealthy, the wealth of pension funds and university endowments and so on. That's what is growing by leaps and bounds.

To see this, we need to name the phenomenon. It can be tracked as the ratio between GDP and financial assets. Bezemer suggests calling this the Unified Financial Assets to Income Ratio, or UNFAIR.[13] In 1995, the UNFAIR ratio was 6:1. In 2020, it approached 10:1. There is ten times more financial wealth than all the activity of the real economy showing up in GDP.

Michael Hudson summed it up in a powerful statement. "What we've described is a whole new way of looking at the economy," he said. "This is a new economic theory."[14]

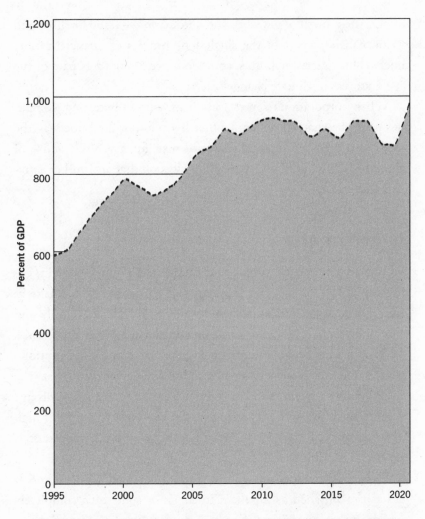

Source: UK Office for National Statistics national accounts data, authors' calculations; Dirk Bezemer, Michael Hudson, and Howard Reed, "Exploring the Capital Gains Economy: The Case of the UK," 2022 unpublished working paper commissioned by the Democracy Collaborative. Included are loans, debt securities, equities, and insurance and pensions.

FIGURE 14.2: UK asset values swell from six times to close to ten times GDP, 1995–2020.

The War Against Labor

Another bit of naming needed is the war against labor. All the skir-mishes of this long war—globalization, outsourcing, the decline of unions, the growth of gig work and automation—could be discussed by journalists as part of the single long process of financialization, much as hurricanes, wildfires, and floods are reported as part of the single process of climate change.

When corporations aggressively fight union organizing, companies could be shamed for antiworker behavior, in the same way the #MeToo movement shamed powerful men for aggressive abuse of women. Calling out bias can break the illusion that antiworker activity is acceptable.

Subversive Acts

Subversive acts can be simple and immediate. Neva Goodwin, co-director of the Global Development and Environment Institute at Tufts University, and also a member of the Rockefeller family and thus an investor, told me how at an institutional investor conference, she "dropped the bomb" of announcing she was capping her portfolio gains. "I told my investment advisor, inflation plus 5 percent, that's the cap. Anything beyond that, I'm going to ask what we're doing wrong," she explained. "It isn't a very stringent cap, especially in a time of high inflation," she told the group. "What's novel, and I think important, is the idea of any limit at all."[15]

How did attendees react? "They looked horrified," she told me. It was as though she'd asked them to consider "something completely outside of their experience." She had, in other words, invited them to awaken.

Board members—or divestment activists in dialogue with boards—might do something similar, asking boards the question I raised in chapter 9: Are portfolio returns too high? MBA students could pose the subversive question in class: Can corporate profits be too high?

Advisors to corporate executives might begin raising the distinction between being profit making and profit maximizing (which I discussed in chapter 5), asking executives: Aren't sustainability changes worth making even if they only break even?

Subversive acts can be as quick as tweets and blog posts. These kinds of acts, along with various forms of pranks and renaming, are gestures that can generate a movement that might accomplish the seemingly impossible. As Edward Said has so provocatively written, decolonization began with active resistance by the colonized and, in the vast majority of cases, that resistance won.[16]

15

THE DEMOCRATIC ECONOMY

Imagining Its Design,
Seeing Its Models Demonstrated

You don't have to see the whole staircase,
just take the first step.

—MARTIN LUTHER KING JR.

AS COLONIZED AS OUR MINDS have been by wealth supremacy, many of us of a progressive bent have forgotten how to hope, how to demand. Our shared imagination has become impoverished.

With chaos mounting, more are realizing that solutions commensurate with the scale of the challenge mean system change. That requires us to get clear on what system change means.

I find myself recalling the story of the Seneca Falls Convention, where one activist dared to suggest women ask for the vote. Lucretia Mott is said to have replied that such a request would make them look ridiculous. They couldn't go that far. Our challenge is to go that far—to begin sharing a vision of what we actually want.

Dreams matter. Visions matter. For better or worse, the collective human mind is a world-shaping force. So too is the human heart—that soul force that has propelled liberatory movements of every kind to their all-but-impossible successes: the abolition movement, votes and rights for women, the global wave of decolonization, and many others. It may be that the ongoing dream of democracy—united with the dreams of preserving the planetary commons and advancing racial equity—together can embody the liberatory force that leads into the next system.

Defining the Democratic Economy

In our book *The Making of a Democratic Economy*, Ted Howard, the cofounder of the Democracy Collaborative, and I defined the democratic economy in these terms:

> A *democratic economy* is an economy of the people, by the people, and for the people. It's an economy that, in its fundamental design, aims to meet the essential needs of all of us, balance human consumption with the regenerative capacity of the earth, respond to the voices and concerns of regular people, and share prosperity without regard to race, gender, national origin, or wealth. At the core of a democratic economy is the common good, in keeping with the founding aims of democracy in politics.[1]

The concept of a democratic economy that Ted and I offered—and that I build out here—is a composite, a synthesis of models and ideas emerging all around us, in response to social pain. The hope is that it offers the beginning of a shared vision, woven from the accomplishments of many who are building what might come next.

Values Form the Heart of System Architecture

As we've seen throughout earlier chapters, economic systems embody simple design elements. Remodeling our system begins with what we *revere*. Values form the moral heart of a social system.

Morality in an economy is something we're taught is unneeded, irrelevant. Possibly embarrassing. Economic decisions are purely rational, mathematical; they're all about self-interest, we're told. The truth is, the extractive economy has a singular morality: *reverence for financial wealth.*

By contrast, the alternate values shared by many include those at the heart of democracy: *liberty, equality, justice.*

Freedom is not just for markets but for all of us. We all belong here, all beings. Nobel Prize–winning economist Amartya Sen describes a redefining of freedom—not as the absence of restraint on powerful economic players, but as the removal of unfreedoms, the removal of poverty and lack of opportunity, bringing people the capability to make meaningful choices about their lives.[2] Philosopher Martha Nussbaum expands this "capabilities approach," saying that a good society is about human dignity, and that to have a life worthy of dignity, we need the capability to pursue it. We need health, freedom to move without fear, political freedom, self-respect, dignified treatment from others.[3]

Beyond the values of democracy, we can recognize other values widely embraced: *sustainability*, a reverence for the living fabric of our common life too long desacralized and desecrated by the industrial economy. *Community*, the ability to care for one another that is essential to a good life, in contrast to the pinched value system of limitless profit seeking for oneself alone. Also *inclusion*, embracing those long excluded—people of color, women, those of different ethnicities. Reparations for historic discrimination lie at the core of democratic economic development, just as making payment for damages is basic to any healthy economy.

These moral values are self-evident. They need not be justified by service to "efficiency" or "productivity" or profit.

Values Define Purpose and Rights

What we value gives rise to system *purpose*. As Donella Meadows emphasized, a system has a set of elements that are connected, organized around a common purpose. The purpose of the democratic economy is the same as the democratic polity: to serve our common good. To allow us to live our lives in freedom, in a system built to be responsive to our needs and voices.

Life-serving purposes are demonstrated in various models we've seen: community-controlled water providing affordable service; a CDFI like BlueHub renegotiating mortgages to serve the disadvantaged. Values and purpose are also brought to life through rights, structures, and forms of governance and accountability that bring democratic principles into the heart of the system—not relying solely on after-the-fact correction through taxation and regulation.

In the economic world envisioned by neoliberals, the rights-bearing citizens are corporations and investors. Democracy is about protecting *human rights and the rights of nature.*

Key to making these a reality is the right relationship of different powers. In the extractive economy, wealth rights are absolute. In the US Constitution, even the president is answerable to the people through elections. The military is subordinate to civilian authority. There's separation of church and state, as well as the separation of powers in the presidency, Congress, and the judiciary. There are limits on the powers of the president, including term limits, the ability of Congress to override a veto, the potential for impeachment and removal. There are limits on the power of government itself in the Bill of Rights. These are all ways to avoid the overbearing power of any individual or group.

In a new paradigm for the economy, the first right relationship is that between the political sphere and the economic sphere. It's a vision of a democratic economy in support of a democratic polity.

Investor rights no longer eclipse all other rights. Labor comes before capital, with worker income no longer a cost to be minimized. In the way debts are handled, there's an imperative for non-humiliation and caring, not ruthlessness.

Among economic human rights taking shape in our time is the emerging *right to water.* The *right to shelter,* recognized in New York state law and elsewhere.[4] A *right to subsistence*, embodied in Social Security for the elderly, beginning to take expanded form in experiments with universal basic income. A *right to education*. Potentially a *right to healthcare*, recognized in the free national health services of many nations, such as the UK. The *right to a living wage*, contested yet increasingly widely embraced.

From Rights to Accountability, Governance, and Infrastructure

In system design, honoring rights and purposes means building in *accountability* to social and ecological outcomes, alongside the financial accountability that economic prudence requires. It means empowering the voices of many in *governance*, as Germany does, for example, in the codetermination practices that govern corporations, where labor is at the table. It means it should be as easy to join a union as it is to join a mutual fund. And it means empowering labor systematically, as, for example, in nationwide sectoral wage bargaining, no longer requiring unions to laboriously proceed shop by shop. It means practicing participatory philanthropy, with the formerly excluded empowered to make decisions on best projects for advancing the democratic economy.

It means new kinds of *infrastructure* for management of investing, for example—shifting from organizations owned overwhelmingly by white men to those owned by women and people of color. It means a new norm of avoiding harm to others through investments.

The overarching infrastructure of the democratic economy is government itself. As economist Mariana Mazucatto has articulated, government today is primed to play a new leading and visionary role, with industrial and financial planning—including managing for inflation, managing financial collapse, and planning for the ecological transition. New national institutions could be created, like Cornell law professor Bob Hockett's idea for a National Reconstruction and Development Council, which would do public planning. Our collective ability to govern ourselves is the bedrock of the good society.

Ownership Evolves

The notion of who matters, who has rights—all of this coalesces in *ownership*. In a democratic economy, wealth is no longer limitless. It would be recognized as a massive system failure if Bill Gates's fortune were to grow, as it has over a quarter century, from roughly $10 billion to more than $130 billion.[5] Once we stopped laughing at how absurd this figure is, we would see this plantation of wealth as outdated, destructive, and a terrible diversion of resources to benefit one man.

From the primitive notion of maximum extraction for oneself, ownership in a democratic economy evolves to a concept of broadly held ownership and stewardship for the good of the whole. Ownership is redesigned for a new era, with water and healthcare systems owned by the public, corporations owned in substantial part by employees, large corporations rechartered to serve the public good, much housing and land and the commons under community control.

These are among the models that have been demonstrated as viable. They enable us to see that a democratic economy works—another element in our theory of change—as the following examples illustrate.

Community-Controlled Land and Housing

One model for land and housing is the *community land trust* (CLT), where the community owns the land, and families own houses on top of it through ninety-nine-year leases. This model protected residents in the financial disaster of 2009, when CLT homes had foreclosure rates below 1 percent, compared to nearly 5 percent for conventionally owned homes.[6] Today this model is protecting against the disaster of climate change.

When Hurricane Ian made landfall in southwest Florida, it caused $67 billion in property damage—yet left unharmed were the twenty-seven cottages of the Florida Keys CLT. These low-energy homes were built atop twelve-foot-tall pilings, meant to withstand wind speeds of two hundred miles per hour. Residents pay just $1,000 a month to live there. This CLT had its genesis after Hurricane Irma, when Maggie Whitcomb and her husband bought damaged properties and placed them in a public trust, blocking a speculative spike in price and building resilience for families hardest hit.[7]

Another example of democratic real estate ownership is the Kensington Corridor Trust. In a racially diverse Philadelphia neighborhood where 58 percent live below the federal poverty line, a mission-driven organization has created a perpetual purpose trust to gain control of a key commercial real estate corridor, ahead of speculators. Using below-market loans from foundations, the trust has acquired fourteen properties, mostly vacant lots and condemned buildings, and is in dialogue with the community on what local businesses to have in those spaces. "Property by property," says Executive Director Adriana Abizadeh, "we're moving to a world where the neighborhood has control."[8]

Community-Controlled Resources, Banking, and a Blockchain Commons

In terms of resources under community control, an important and widespread model is the municipal electric utility. In Omaha, Nebraska, voters elect the utility board, board meetings are open to the public and televised, and each year a portion of profits are returned to the city budget. Community-owned electric utilities serve more than forty-nine million Americans and are documented to provide better service at lower rates than investor-owned utilities. The entire state of Nebraska is powered by cooperatives and municipal utilities.[9]

In terms of banking, there's a growing movement for city- and state-owned banks, like those being explored by Philadelphia, San Francisco, and elsewhere, which build on the hundred-year history of the state-owned Bank of North Dakota; it supported small-business lending in that state through the 2008 downturn, even as big banks elsewhere had stopped doing so.

The spirit of designing for fairness and the common good is entering the blockchain world as well, with my friends Gideon Rosenblatt, a former Microsoft executive, and Nathan Schneider, introduced in chapter 14, both involved in bringing good governance to blockchain technology. Rosenblatt told me he's working with a group to build a Token Engineering Commons, a global commons with a goal of becoming "a network to create ethical, safe economic systems." He sees it "as the new economic fabric," a way to resist the autocratic temptations of technologies like Facebook and now Twitter, instead allowing decentralized coordination. In his words, "With the world we may be going into and the growing risks of authoritarianism, this may be a lifeline."

Broad-Based Ownership through Cooperatives, Worker Ownership

In terms of demonstrations of workable democratic economy models, most extensive of all is the worldwide system of cooperatives, which are owned by the people they serve, like the depositor-owned credit unions in the US, which have more than $2 trillion in assets.[10]

There's also a movement for platform cooperatives, where gig workers take control of their fate by cutting out the Silicon Valley middlemen and owning their own company, giving them direct say in their pay and benefits. One such example is the Driver's Cooperative, launched in New York City in 2021, which now has six thousand members.[11]

There are six thousand substantially worker-owned ESOP companies in the US. Examples include Recology, a recycling and waste hauling company based in San Francisco with more than $1 billion in revenue, which is 100 percent owned by its workers and whose stated purpose is creating "a world without waste." Garbage truck drivers there can make six-figure salaries, because when there are no absentee shareholders extracting profits, there's more to go around for workers.[12]

In another instance, a new kind of staffing agency is solving the problem of the disaggregated workforce while also benefiting workers who are predominantly people of color. AlliedUp is a worker-owned healthcare staffing cooperative, incubated by SEIU–United Healthcare Workers West, which places unionized healthcare workers in jobs. In some states, 76 percent of healthcare workers are women of color. The cooperative is a way to enable workers to own the staffing agency that employs them—when they don't own the hospitals and health systems where they're sent every day. AlliedUp placed one thousand workers in its first year and aims to recruit another three thousand by the end of 2023 (*AlliedUp.com/*).

Corporations Redesigned to Serve the Public Good

All of these models could be advanced through a great ownership transition, making democratic ownership a larger and larger part of the landscape over time, through a process my colleague Gar Alperovitz terms "evolutionary reconstruction."

But even if all of these democratic models were to grow substantially, it would not eliminate today's traditional corporations; indeed, those massive companies might well absorb successful change efforts, or thwart them. How can corporations be redesigned? It's not wise to make the goal eliminating all private property, as communism envisioned, or eliminating all private enterprise. Certainly, more public ownership is needed, with whole new sectors—like health and water and education—ideally brought under public ownership and control. Yet private enterprise is also vital. The imperative of our age is that it evolve into a new form.

The challenge is to envision, and create, private enterprises and investing processes that *remove capital bias*. Enterprises may still be profit making; that's an imperative of staying in business. What is dangerous, as outlined in chapter 5, is the unfettered aim of profit *maximizing*.

The redesign of corporations and capital markets is relatively uncharted territory for progressives, some of whom may see any notion of profit or private enterprise as inherently capitalist, or see private investing as necessarily extractive.

The concept is to re-envision enterprises not as objects owned by external shareholders, but as living systems, human communities, subsystems of the earth. As economist Kate Raworth, author of *Doughnut Economics*, and her colleague Erinch Sahan of the Doughnut Economics Action Lab (*DoughnutEconomics.org*) put it, we need enterprises that are redistributive and regenerative by design. Using concepts of ownership structure I articulated in my book *Owning Our Future*, they've created a tool to help companies navigate toward deep redesign that is now being used by companies and business schools around the world.[13]

Corporate redesign is a topic that could easily fill an entire book, indeed many books; it's something I've written about extensively, beginning with *The Divine Right of Capital* in 2001, which Jay Coen Gilbert told me inspired him—along with Andrew Kassoy and Bart Houlahan—to create the concept of the *B Corporation*, a model of business as a force for good. In the B Corporation, we can glimpse a microcosm that helps us imagine how transformational change might advance.

It begins with mostly smaller, founder-led companies adopting legal requirements to serve many stakeholders in governing documents. This is what nineteen B Corporation pioneers did in 2007. Today there are some five thousand certified B Corporations across 79 countries and 154 industries, including firms like Patagonia, Cooperative Home Care Associates, and Beneficial State Bank (*BCorporation.net*). Best among them are the dozens of enterprises that are both B Corporations and worker owned, which my colleagues and I have called next-generation private enterprises.

The concept of B Corporations next broadened to become a legal form of state incorporation, today available in thirty-six states, with thousands of companies adopting it, including Plum Organics and Kickstarter.[14] The idea could also serve as the seed concept for federal legislation creating a new kind of responsible major corporation, redesigned in its structures of power.

That's the aim of policy proposed by Senator Elizabeth Warren in her Accountable Capitalism Act, which would require corporations with more than $1 billion in revenue to obtain a new federal corporate charter. That innovative charter would require corporate directors to consider all major corporate stakeholders—not only shareholders—in company decisions. It also would give workers a strong voice, with employees electing at least 40 percent of directors.[15]

What we can see evolving in these various efforts is a new concept of the company as a just firm, designed from the inside out for a new mandate: to serve broad well-being and the public good. The just firm is the only kind that should ultimately be permitted to exist.[16]

If these kinds of enterprise ownership and governance changes seem arcane, they are potentially potent ways to reduce financial extraction systemwide, redistributing trillions of dollars to broad public benefit and to workers. Effective corporate redesign can accomplish this without government spending, instead having government serve as system designer.

Prototyping the Future

While some of these models are substantial and well developed, others are new and small. Doesn't everything start small? What became today's Social Security system began as experiments in Montana and Nevada as they grappled with aiding the elderly. These became prototypes for the massive national system that in 2022 distributed Social Security benefits of over $1 trillion to sixty-six million Americans.[17]

Similarly in Britain, the National Health Service created in 1948 drew inspiration from the Tredegar Medical Aid Society, a community-based medical aid system in South Wales begun by workers banding together to provide services for their families, later serving most of the town by offering medical, pharmacy, dental, and other services all "free at the point of use." When Clement Atlee's government was elected in a landslide, this small Welsh experiment proved a model for the creation of one of the world's great national health systems.

———

Seeing these various approaches and models, we can begin to imagine the mosaic of a different kind of economy in the making—a system whose institutions *in their normal functioning* create broad well-being.

Yet there's a final question unaddressed: a next system for capital. Is it theoretically possible that an entire system of sophisticated, modern finance could serve the public good? This was a question I set out to explore one summer as I brought together experts who were pursuing various strands of work and had already figured out a good many answers, and whose work, in aggregate, seemed to add up to a full next system of capital.

16

DEMOCRATIZING
FINANCE

*Pathways Toward a
Next System of Capital*

I HAD THE GOOD fortune, in early 2022, to hear ecological economist Herman Daly speak at a Tellus Institute salon, where I and a
dozen or so other Tellus fellows were able to talk with this visionary
genius in person. He was warm and at ease, and spoke of how chas-
tened he felt by the fact that his ideas of the low-growth or no-growth
economy had been ignored, all his life, by the mainstream of his pro-
fession. Our time with him was only eight months before his death.

One metaphor Professor Daly used will always stay with me.
He spoke of how our economy, in its approach to consumption and
economic growth, lacks any concept of a Plimsoll line, that mark on
the hull of a ship indicating how heavily it can be loaded before it's
swamped, at risk of sinking.[1]

I came away thinking that we also lack a Plimsoll line for finance—
a notion of how many capital claims can be loaded upon the backs
of people and society before our economy becomes catastrophically
destabilized. How massive can financial extraction be before the social
order itself becomes unworkable?

We face two kinds of overgrowth, consumption and finance, which intertwine in a vicious cycle. Target and Walmart don't push us to buy more Saran Wrap and plastic forks because they care if we use more forks, but because they care about growing the bottom line, which keeps share price growing, which makes CEOs rich through stock options; a rising share price also pleases shareholders and keeps CEOs from being fired. Capital—that money which must always grow—is in the driver's seat. The growth of consumption is the result.

Poet Gary Snyder wrote about the "growth monster" whose relentless expansion imperils many species, asking, "If the lad or lass is among us who knows where the secret heart of this Growth Monster is hidden," please tell us where to shoot the arrow to slow it down.[2]

That secret heart is capital. Where we shoot the arrow is into *the idea* of capital. The centerless mindset. The paradigm.

A next system of capital begins with a simple premise:

> We cannot continue to operate our economy based on maximum growth of capital.

That was the starting premise on the table as my colleagues and I gathered fifteen people for a July 22, 2022, meeting at Boston University's Global Development Policy Center. Our aim was to explore a set of pathways that, as a whole, would offer a starting sketch of how to move toward a full next system of capital.

In our theory of system change, pathways build upon models, adding a next step: describing how we begin to get from here to there—in this case, from the extractive system of finance to a system of democratized finance.

Our meeting took inspiration from the Stabilization Wedges approach to carbon mitigation developed by Princeton researchers Stephen Pacala and Robert Socolow, which has become a paradigm for its field. Given the enormous task of reducing greenhouse gas emissions, the wedges showed how growing use of green energy approaches—wind, solar, carbon capture, and so on—could rec greenhouse gas concentration. In one diagram, the wedges helped us to imagine that the impossible was possible, utilizing tools and ideas already available.

We aimed to do something comparable: to show how growing use of existing democratic finance approaches could reduce wealth concentration. The result of our exploration is the seven pathways shown in figure 16.1.

All seven approaches would work together to ensure capital would no longer be in control but in service to life. Yet with any complex system, change can begin anywhere, radiating out in unexpected ways. For example, debt jubilee—debt forgiveness—holds the power to jolt us: You mean all debts don't always have to be paid? Such awakening, spurred by one pathway, can make other pathways seem suddenly more feasible.

The meeting advanced a number of points of system change: helping *imagine* a next system; showing how various approaches have been *demonstrated* as workable; and laying out the *pathways* by which we might, over time—and beginning now—build a financial system that distributes capital in a way that is just, sustainable, and non-extractive, as a necessary part of the architecture of a democratic economy.

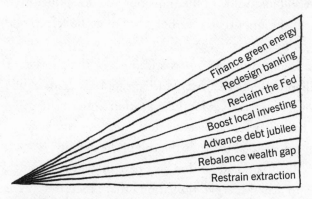

FIGURE 16.1: Seven pathways to reduce wealth concentration

Working with my colleague Leslie Harroun, senior fellow for strategic initiatives, with research support from Amy Gluckman, former editor at *Dollars and Sense*, we searched out transformative work underway in different aspects of finance, and structured the meeting by putting on the table the seven pathways, bringing together experts who could address each. By the end of the meeting, our rudimentary starting ideas had developed into robust pathway descriptions, with clear concepts of the public good that each would serve. It began to look like something approaching a comprehensive set of pathways to a next system of capital:

1. **Finance the energy transition** in ways that democratize power and ownership.

   We met during a week when England was under a "red" warning for extreme heat for the first time in history—a week when temperatures in London soared above 100 degrees and the London Luton airport shut down temporarily because the tarmac was melting. I kept an eye on this as the day for the gathering approached, because one attendee from London had hoped to fly in but instead chose to attend by Zoom.

   That attendee was Mark Campanale, founder of Carbon Tracker, known for linking the established concept of "stranded assets" to the carbon budget, to show the substantial level of assets that will lose value in the transition to a fossil fuel–free economy, all the unburnable carbon that must be left in the ground if civilization is to survive.

   As Mark joined us, news was still fresh of the passage of Biden's Inflation Reduction Act, which created hundreds of billions of dollars in incentives for the transition to green energy—a package that analysts said would cut US carbon emissions to 40 percent below 2005 levels by the end of the decade.[3]

   Mark talked about how this was part of a breakthrough approach to the energy transition that theorists were embracing—not putting carbon taxes on dirty energy, which was the old consensus, but instead using policy incentives to make the clean stuff cheaper. I found myself thinking, yes, this is an example of government shifting from a regulatory approach to becoming system designer, influencing how capital flows.

We've been living in a false narrative, Mark said, where the old system told us the clean energy transition would be expensive and impractical. In truth it will save us money. Green energy is now cheaper than fossil fuels, he emphasized. Really the issue is that maximized profits by fossil fuel producers are threatened.[4]

"In this new energy system, all the flows are essentially free," he said. Once you've bought your wind or solar infrastructure and it pays for itself, you're using free inputs of wind and sun. You're no longer dependent on fossil fuels from large corporations, which disrupts their oligopolistic position as suppliers.

"Two things happen," Mark said. "First, concentration of wealth in energy corporations disappears. Second, energy gets low in cost. Super profits disappear as costs lower."

"Instead of centralized, concentrated power, you have distributed energy at the village level, household level, town level," he said. You can have energy ownership by local companies, cooperatives. It could be a way of redistributing wealth to historically disadvantaged communities, he added.

What also might happen in the future, he continued, is that oligarchical wealth—the Saudis, Russia, Charles Koch—loses power. "We could see a transformation of power," Mark said.

But all this depends on who gets to *own* the next system of energy. Large corporations could easily retain ownership over distributed power. Local, democratic ownership needs to be a deliberate part of the energy transition. We see here again the foundational power of ownership. That and the other elements of system design—like purpose, accountability, governance, and infrastructure—recurred throughout the meeting.

2. **Develop an ecosystem of banking** and finance designed from the start to work in the public interest.

We heard from my colleague Stephanie McHenry, CEO of the Democracy Collaborative and former president of Shore-Bank Cleveland, the for-profit, mission-led bank that once did high-touch lending in her predominantly Black neighborhood. Stephanie spoke of how the community she'd been helping was damaged by the subprime lenders who moved in before the 2008 crisis. We need an expanded system of community capital, she said, including far greater support for CDFIs.

My colleague Joe Guinan, president of the Democracy Collaborative, shared the UK research he'd commissioned from Dirk Bezemer, Michael Hudson, and Howard Reed, discussed in earlier chapters. Joe talked about financialization—sketching out how an alternative, comprehensive banking system would make serving human needs its *purpose*. In Joe's words, "we need a top-to-bottom ecosystem of mutual, cooperative, community, and public banks that would be focused entirely on investment in the real economy, in greening production, in providing jobs, retirement security, and an economy of real human needs."

Central to this vision is the growing movement for more public banks. As a prereading before the event, we circulated the ideas of Cornell Law professor Robert Hockett, who envisions an integrated network of state and regional public banks, with lenders of various kinds expanded or created that are responsive to public input and serve community needs. These entities could also be responsible for large-scale investments in the public interest, including research and development, infrastructure, clean energy, and energy conservation.[5]

One example is Fannie Mae, a government-sponsored finance entity created by Congress that now deploys private capital. Fannie and its cousin, Freddie Mac, are responsible for more than 60 percent of mortgages in the US. Had they refused to purchase predatory loans and remained true to their original *purpose*—to serve homeowners and expand housing on fair terms—they might have lessened the breadth and severity of the mortgage meltdown. *Governance* in the public interest, including consumer-oriented board members, might have made a difference. Also needed was democratic *accountability*, with CEO pay tied not to share price metrics, as it was at Fannie Mae, but to social metrics.[6]

Fannie Mae is an example of how government shaping of capital flows need not mean writing checks out of the Treasury. It can instead back private capital via loan guarantees, other credit subsidies, or secondary market purchasing of loans to influence the structures and terms for capital to flow. This is what Biden is doing with clean energy incentives.

It could be done so as to support a flow of money into converting companies to employee ownership—building that alternative conveyor belt we need, so that fewer companies end up in the hands of big capital. That's the approach proposed with the Employee Equity Investment Act, for example, a policy idea that proposes Small Business Administration–type backing for equity funds that transition firms to worker ownership.[7]

3. **Reclaim the Federal Reserve** and create national coordination for productive community development.

The Federal Reserve was initially set up to serve a large national network of locally rooted banks, few of which remain today, after the neoliberal revolution of the 1980s and 1990s allowed megabanks to swallow up the small banks. When banks left low-income communities, vulture lenders—payday lenders, tax refund lenders—moved in, and private equity is now invested in some of the largest of these.

Our demands to democratize finance ought to be much more radical than they typically are, Hockett argues. He suggests reimagining the Federal Reserve, which now serves the big banks, as the people's Fed, a "bank of the people." Regional offices of the Fed could revive their old function of financing economic development by purchasing the loans and bonds of private enterprises, with a purpose of serving public priorities.[8]

Hockett also proposes a National Reconstruction and Development Council as a strategic planning board, analogous to the War Industries Board and War Finance Corporation of World War I, and similar bodies in WWII. This body would bear primary responsibility for projecting and overseeing productive national investment, creating an annual development strategy while coordinating funding for projects, such as infrastructure.

4. **Shift investment from Wall Street to Main Street** to create jobs and community wealth that nurture the real economy.

We also heard from Michael Shuman, author of *Put Your Money Where Your Life Is* and publisher of *Main Street Journal*. He talked about massively shifting investment to local, community-enhancing purposes. He spoke about the paradox that 60 to 80 percent of jobs are with locally rooted businesses and institutions (like public schools and hospitals), yet most investment is nonlocal. Nearly all our long-term investment (stocks, corporate bonds, mutual funds, pensions, insurance funds) goes into publicly traded vehicles remote from communities. Trillions of dollars flow to Wall Street, while local firms are starved for capital.

"ESG is just a distraction and doesn't change this dynamic," Michael said with frustration. It's accelerating our movement on the wrong track, when we need to jump to a different track altogether.

We talked about how the (at one time) rising stock values on Wall Street had been inflated by stock buybacks—artificially boosting prices and contributing to the bubble that burst. "In moments of collapse, our job is to *prevent* a rescue," Michael urged. Instead of bailing out this system, as we did in 2009, or saving the large utilities demanding help, "we have to figure out how to kill them gracefully or transform them into something else."

We saw in chapter 14 how few dollars "invested" in publicly traded companies actually reach companies for productive use. Michael's work shows how local investing, by contrast, is productive investment that builds family firms, aids entrepreneurs, creates jobs, and keeps real estate wealth local.

Fortunately, state and local governments are beginning to aid this shift. For example, the Connecticut Green Bank's offering of $25 million in Green Liberty Bonds—issued to further its mission of reducing climate change—sold out in forty-eight hours.[9] Michael emphasized that Republicans also often support local investing, creating the potential for a left/right coalition in building this pathway.

New system *infrastructure* is needed to support more local investment. New kinds of exchanges, for example, could support local investing. Yet while we've built superhighways for speculative investments, productive local investments currently travel dirt paths. What we need, Michael said, is a generation of innovative young finance people to figure it all out—the kind of young people he encounters as he teaches in the Bard Green MBA program.

Much of that innovation is beginning to come at warp speed from the impact investing world, where countless funds invest in marginalized communities, decarbonize buildings, advance sustainable development goals, build asset ownership in BIPOC (Black, Indigenous, and people of color) communities, and accomplish infinitely more.

One leader in transformational community investing, for example, is Nwamaka Agbo, who leads the San Francisco–based

Kataly Foundation, cofounded by Regan Pritzker, that works to bring ownership and control of assets to BIPOC communities. They've invested, for example, in the East Bay Permanent Real Estate Cooperative, which helps convert real estate into cooperative housing for existing tenants. Agbo began initially with a focus on green jobs. But then the recognition dawned that "we should have been dreaming bigger," Agbo said. "We should have been positioning ourselves as the ones to be the business owners, to be the designers, the architects and the decision-makers."[10]

5. **Advance the debt jubilee** to create economic stability, alleviate burdens, and aid ecosystems.

Another pathway on the list for our Boston group was the idea of a debt jubilee, seen, for example, in Biden's proposed forgiveness of student loan debt. The story of debt is really the story of the dispossessed. It's the underside of the property regime, since much of the burden imposed by finance on ordinary people is in the form of debt.

Wiping away debt has been the great unthinkable idea. It now needs to become thinkable.

Michael Hudson argues that when debts grow too large to be paid without ruining debtors, canceling bad debts is the way to restore balance and renew the economy. After WWII, for example, when most of Germany was insolvent, a debt jubilee through currency reform wiped out 90 percent of government and private debt. Germany emerged virtually debt free, paving the way for the "Miracle on the Rhine," the nation's rapid reconstruction that helped make it the powerhouse it is today.[11]

One of the most striking forms of debt cancellation is the debt-for-nature swap, discussed by one of our participants, doctoral candidate Pamela Icyeza, who is researching how capital market participation has affected sub-Saharan African states. She's a research fellow at Boston University's Global Development Policy Center, which hosted our event.

In one recent debt-for-nature swap, completed in 2021, Belize was able to reduce its external debt by an impressive 10 percent of GDP; $553 million in debt sold for 55 cents on the dollar (which meant the other 45 cents of each dollar of debt was wiped out). The deal was arranged by the Nature Conservancy, financed by private investors, underwritten by Credit Suisse, and insured by the International Development Finance Corporation, which meant even risk-averse pension funds could feel confident of repayment. In return for the debt reduction, Belize will spend millions each year on marine conservation, enabling it to double its marine-protection parks, which span coral reefs, mangroves, fish spawning grounds, and areas filled with sea grasses.[12]

Debt-for-nature swaps represent a shift in how lenders think about risk and value. That is, given the growing awareness of the systemic economic (and thus financial) risks of climate change and biodiversity loss, there's value in preserving nature and reducing climate change. Investors see reduction in debt repayment as being compensated for by reduced systemic risk.

Debt jubilee has powerful potential for movement building for the democratic economy. In the UK, the concept is being advanced by the grassroots group Debt Justice, which seeks to relieve the debt burden of countries like Pakistan. In the US, it's advanced by the Debt Collective, a debtors' union working to cancel debts and organize debt strikes; it was this group, arising out of Occupy Wall Street, that put student loan forgiveness on the political map. The Debt Collective (*DebtCollective.org*) says its movement has abolished billions in student debt, medical debt, payday loans, probation debt, and credit card debt.

There is a strong moral argument for debt relief. The word *jubilee* comes from the Hebrew word for trumpet, *yobel*. In Mosaic Law, the trumpet was blown every fifty years to start the Year of the Lord, in which personal debts were canceled. The Gospel of Luke describes Jesus unrolling the scroll of

Isaiah and saying he had come to announce the Year of the Lord, the Jubilee Year.[13]

In this spirit, more than 460 churches have worked with RIP Medical Debt to forgive medical debt. The group was the brainchild of two former debt collectors, Craig Antico and Jerry Ashton, whose business model had been based on buying debt at a deep discount, then pushing borrowers to repay and pocketing the difference. In conversation with debt justice advocates, they realized they could simply forgive this debt, using philanthropic dollars to do so. They founded RIP Medical Debt to carry out this idea. Thus it is that churches can now work with this nonprofit to purchase debt for as low as a penny on the dollar—$1 buying $100—and then simply notify people that their debt is gone. RIP Medical Debt has so far wiped out $6.7 billion in medical debt.[14]

Yet debt erasure alone doesn't create a just system. Bernie Sanders proposed eliminating medical debt, then creating a universal healthcare system to prevent it from building again.[15]

6. **Rebalance the intergenerational wealth gap** with wealth taxes and baby bonds.

In a democratic economy, wealth would neither be vastly concentrated nor completely eliminated. Instead, *ownership* of assets would be spread more democratically. The old "rights" of wealth holders to limitless returns in perpetuity would give way to the human rights of ordinary people. The transmission of economic advantage or disadvantage across generations would be systematically diminished. Inheritance and wealth taxes are democratic tools to eliminate the massive, intergenerational financial dynasties that create undemocratic power. While reasonable levels of inheritance could continue, billionaire empires would no longer be possible.

The people most powerfully advancing the idea of wealth taxes are wealthy themselves, like Marlene Engelhorn, cofounder of the group Tax Me Now. This thirty-something heir is one in a growing number of leftist youth millionaires advocating for higher taxes on wealth, gathering in groups like Patriotic Millionaires and Resource Generation.[16]

At the other end of the continuum, it's also vital to increase the assets of those without wealth—a goal being pursued through *baby bonds*, a concept discussed at our gathering by Grieve Chelwa, the Inaugural Postdoctoral Fellow at the Institute on Race, Power, and Political Economy at the New School. He joined our group by Zoom from Zambia.

Baby bonds are publicly funded trust accounts that give every child, at birth, a financial nest egg to help them attain financial security when they reach adulthood. They showcase a pathway to evening out the common inheritance of society, regardless of the race, gender, and economic circumstance in which a child is born.[17]

"The typical US Black household has 12 cents for every dollar a white household has," Grieve said. As baby bonds close that gap, they are an antiracist policy. In words echoing those of philosopher Martha Nussbaum, Grieve emphasized that in the absence of inclusive economic rights, people have limited capacity to meet their material needs. "Inclusive economic rights take us closer to a moral economy," he said.

The baby bond idea has been introduced at the federal level in the US with the American Opportunity Accounts Act. Both Connecticut and Washington, DC, have created baby bonds programs.

7. **Restrain financial extraction** by reining in private equity/ hedge funds and mobilizing institutional investors.

If we make only positive ideas the heart of building a democratic economy, everything we build will continue to be devoured. We must take on extraction itself. Most urgently, that means taking on the apex predator of private equity.

There's a growing sophistication on the left about private equity. An example is the Climate Risk Scorecard project created by the Private Equity Stakeholder Project and Americans for Financial Reform Education Fund. As private equity snaps up and keeps alive the dirty fossil fuel assets being discarded by big oil (as we saw in chapter 9), these groups are mobilizing to push back. Their scorecard project is built on the premise that we can't afford to let private equity pollute "under the shroud of darkness" and put people's retirement at risk. The scorecard examines eight PE firms with a combined $3.6 trillion AUM, rating their energy holdings on indicators such as downstream carbon dioxide emissions. The group makes a clear set of demands, which include meeting science-based climate targets and reporting on a portfolio-wide energy transition plan.[18]

One aim of the scorecard project is educating institutional investors to make demands of their PE partners. Educating institutional investors is also the work of the Predistribution Initiative's Delilah Rothenberg, who spoke at our gathering about how the migration of institutional funds into PE funds is creating unseen systemic risks for the economy as a whole. The Predistribution Initiative also works with investors to develop regenerative PE structures, which create more balanced wealth distribution.[19]

Reining in private equity, comprehensively, will take something like the Stop Wall Street Looting Act introduced in 2019 by Senator Elizabeth Warren and others, which would restrain private equity in various ways. Yet the more immediate work of educating institutional investors is powerful in itself, as it begins to drive a wedge into the maximizing mind, helping trustees and directors tangibly see that high returns do not fall unblemished from the sky, and that they themselves as asset owners, by moving their assets up that risk–return spectrum and consolidating capital with the largest asset managers, are abetting the fracturing of society and planet all around us.

These seven pathways, taken as a whole and working together cata-lytically, begin to show how an entire next system of capital might be possible. If we hold the idea of these pathways in our mind, imagining how they could multiply the combined energy of many visionaries, the impossible begins to seem—well, if not immediately *possible*, at least *imaginable*. And that's a start.

17

BEGINNING
WHERE YOU LIVE

Building Community Wealth

HIS SCOTTISH BROGUE IS SO THICK that it's sometimes hard for me to understand him, but his enthusiasm is unmistakably infectious. This is a man on fire. Neil McInroy is just back from a two-week-long barnstorming trip through Australia, meeting with officials from Sydney and Melbourne, attending an Australian Labor Party dinner, teaching master classes to economic development professionals, speaking with a large pension authority, and more. In his seemingly countless meetings, Neil's topic was one and the same: *community wealth building* (CWB), a form of local economic development that transforms local economies through communities having direct ownership and control of their assets.

Neil is global lead fellow at the Democracy Collaborative, working closely with Sarah McKinley, director of CWB programs—the two of them a formidable pair of Johnny Appleseeds spreading the story of building community wealth. As Sarah explains, this form of economic development takes the various models of the democratic economy—such as community land trusts, worker-owned firms, and public banks—and connects them in place, building infrastructures of support to scale and supercharge these efforts, so they work together as *a system*.[1]

Communities Looking for Alternatives

"This is not just a small pilot project here and there," Neil says. "This is about rewiring the economy for social, economic, and ecological justice."[2]

If the idea of a full-fledged democratic economy takes shape first in the imagination, it's being demonstrated in tangible communities—most often, communities suffering from decades of disinvestment and disempowerment. These are the seedbed of what could come next in the project of bringing the economy back to earth, designing it to benefit ordinary people. It starts in our own backyards.

For these communities, the necessity of system change is already a painful lived reality. What community wealth brings them is proven models demonstrated as effective, and the imaginative vision of an entire local economy functioning in a new way, keeping wealth recirculating locally.

The concept of CWB, first articulated by the Democracy Collaborative in 2005, has today developed a momentum all its own—and it's being aided by a variety of organizations, like the Centre for Local Economic Strategies in the UK. In addition to the UK, the idea is catching on in cities like Amsterdam, Copenhagen, and Barcelona, as well as in US areas like Chicago; Alameda County, California; and Somerville, Massachusetts. New interest is coming from places as far-flung as Poland, South Korea, Germany, and Bordeaux in France.

"Globally, there's a recognition that the economic system is not working properly. Capitalism is in disarray," Neil told me. "Many state and local authorities are looking for alternatives."[3]

In Chicago—the third largest city in the US, where six in ten residents are Black and brown—a $15 million CWB pilot was created by former Mayor Lori Lightfoot, and it's being led by the Office of

Equity and Racial Justice. Among its goals are narrowing the wealth gap and stabilizing neighborhoods. [4]

A Nation Takes on Community Wealth Building

On the largest scale, one country is taking a whole-nation approach—Scotland, where Neil serves as a CWB advisor. The Scottish government has named a Minister of Public Finance, Planning and Community Wealth Building, and it's financially supporting CWB in a series of places, with additional supportive legislation in the works. At the forefront is North Ayrshire, an area of 130,000 and one of Scotland's hardest-hit communities, which has made community wealth the central focus of all its economic development. Following its lead, all local councils across the country will be developing CWB plans.[5]

The North Ayrshire council has designated a number of staff to work on CWB, advised by a Community Wealth Building Commission of local stakeholders. The council's strategy embraces the various pillars of CWB: progressive procurement, just use of land and property, fair work, locally rooted finance, and inclusive and democratic enterprise. The city is investing in net-zero emissions by 2030, building two city-owned solar farms on former landfill sites, which will be operated as a municipal enterprise. These could potentially produce more than twice the energy needed for all municipal buildings, including schools, with excess energy sold to local anchor institutions. It's an example of combining the just use of land, democratic enterprise, local investment, and anchor procurement.[6]

Another example of land use is a large-scale woodland tree planting program aimed at providing carbon absorption and other community benefits.[7] In terms of progressive procurement, local anchor institutions—the local council, college, police and fire services—have signed onto an anchor charter, pledging to buy and invest locally. This has enabled an organic farm in East Ayrshire, Mossgiel Farm, to supply local organic milk to schools. And, as the farmer says, the children "can visit my farm and see where their food comes from." The city council has also worked with local employers to adopt fair work practices and to create a program of forty apprenticeships for youth. As larger infrastructure projects proceed, they'll emphasize contracting with local businesses, including cooperatives, and providing quality jobs that pay a living wage.[8]

A Game Changer for Worker Ownership

In its work supporting democratic enterprise, North Ayrshire is encouraging family-owned businesses to consider converting to worker ownership. An impressive example was the sale of Auchrannie, a resort on the nearby Isle of Arran, to its employees. The complex, which includes two hotels and three restaurants, is valued at £4.3 million. Full ownership is now held in an employee ownership trust on behalf of the resort's 160 employees. The former owners will be paid out of company profits over twenty-five years.[9]

In Cleveland, where CWB first began with the creation of three Evergreen Cooperatives—including the anchor-supported Evergreen Cooperative Laundry—this network of worker cooperatives has expanded into converting other local businesses to worker ownership through its Fund for Employee Ownership. Jessica Rose, a former colleague at the Democracy Collaborative and now the chief financial officer at the Global Impact Investing Network, and I aided in developing the concept of such a fund, and Jessica worked on launching the strategic fund, which is now overseen by Evergreen's chief investment officer, Jeanette Webster. We discovered a dozen similar funds forming across the US, and we published research on them.[10]

One fund that I was particularly excited to celebrate was Apis & Heritage Capital Partners, which has a targeted focus of using worker ownership to build wealth for BIPOC workers. It was incubated by the Democracy at Work Institute and launched by cofounders Todd Leverette, Philip Reeves, and Michael Brownrigg, beginning with an initial $30 million from investors such as the Ford, Skoll, and

Rockefeller Foundations. When this fund converted Apex Plumbing of Denver and Accent Landscape Contractors of El Paso, Texas, to 100 percent employee ownership, it was majority Latino workforces of 150 workers that benefited—along with the exiting owners and the fund's investors.[11]

Could expanding funds like this serve as an alternative to the conveyor belt perpetually feeding firms into the mouth of big capital? If these funds grew and caught on, could they form a potentially substantial pathway toward a democratic economy?

Investment banker Dick May, with American Working Capital, believes they could. He and his colleague Chris Mackin conceived the original idea of the proposed policy of the Employee Equity Investment Act, mentioned in the previous chapter, designed to bring Small Business Administration–type backing for worker ownership conversion funds. They estimate that in a decade, an annual federal loan guarantee commitment of $100 billion could create thirteen million new worker owners—roughly *double* the number of worker owners today. To call this a game changer is a dramatic understatement. It would be transformative.[12]

Clearly, a game changer is needed. The number of ESOP firms has been declining for two decades, down from 9,200 in 1995 to 6,500 today (though plan participants have increased).[13] Only about two hundred firms a year now convert to an ESOP.[14] That's a drop in the ocean compared to the seventeen thousand traditional mergers and acquisitions made in 2020.[15]

Turning this around would take the clout of the federal government. It might also take the development of different models, or changes to ESOP law, or other financial innovations.

It doesn't seem immediately likely. It would take time. But it could happen. As Neil said, communities are looking for alternatives. So are investors.

Improbable change happens all the time.

"What's Happening Blew My Mind"

One group of folks not waiting on federal action are the activists in Amarillo, Texas, who have replicated the Evergreen Cooperative Laundry concept in the Texas panhandle. It's one of the reddest areas in the country, and an area also known for "the Panhandle spirit," a spirit of caring and community that makes it a place many can't imagine leaving. A worker-owned commercial laundry is up and running now, located on land from the city, with construction funding from the Amarillo Area Foundation and a consortium of locally owned banks, all with very generous repayment terms.

The Amarillo group is now working on a larger CWB initiative. When they hosted a lunch to explore the idea, thirty-eight people showed up, including fifteen members of the local chamber of commerce and a leader from Bank of America. Fully twenty-eight said they wanted to continue the conversation. "The timing is right," said my friend Mary, a core member of the activist group.[16]

She spoke excitedly about discovering that Amarillo had four worker-owned or cooperative companies, like Cactus Feeders with its eight hundred employee owners. It also has a community land trust, Mariposa Village (*Mariposa.eco*), which hosts the Mariposa Tech Co-op of aspiring technology creators. A community-owned grocery is in the works in the region. And there's a woman interested in starting a fund to support women-owned businesses.

"Seeing what's happening in Amarillo blew my mind," Mary said. We talked about the "silver tsunami" of 3 million retiring baby boomer business owners in the US and how most of these businesses could close, yet selling to workers was a way to keep these businesses and their jobs going, recirculating local wealth. When she shared this idea with the pastor of a local Latino church, he told her he had a lot of those business owners in his congregation, people like plumbers and electricians, whose children didn't want to take over their companies; employees could be the logical new owners. The Amarillo group is interested in starting an employee ownership center, and I connected them with the Employee Ownership Expansion Network, which is starting state centers across the country, with a network of twenty so far.

"This isn't about pushing a boulder up a hill," Mary said. "We're at the top of the hill. We need to push the boulder down."

She'd read various drafts of my book in progress, and she told me it was pointing to something so clear: "Once you see it, you can't unsee it." But, she urged, "don't leave people in despair. There's more happening than people know, and I suspect that's true all over. We're not starting from zero. This is the beginning."

CONCLUSION

We're Not Talking about the Real Problem Yet

> *We live in capitalism. Its power seems inescapable. So did the divine right of kings. Any human power can be resisted and changed by human beings.*
>
> —URSULA K. LE GUIN

THERE'S A REASON that wealth supremacy—capital bias, property bias—has lagged behind other forms of bias in being recognized. The end of a property regime is the end of a way of life. The end of the property regime of slavery and plantations was the end of a way of life in the American South. The end of the property regime of imperialism was the end of an age.

A way of life on our planet is ending. Whether we find our way out of the chaos to positive system change remains to be seen.

Yes, we have to work on positive solutions, building community wealth, advancing employee ownership, and much more. My work for the last three decades has been about little else. But I've come to see that we also—and, I'd argue, first—have to grapple with the scale and depth of the problem. In order for the work of building alternatives to take on the enormous momentum it requires, we need to recognize our situation as an emergency. Not just the emergency of climate change and the polycrisis. The emergency of financialization. The unrelenting problem of too much financial extraction, the way this is locked in because the unseen ruling class has our society in a stranglehold, quietly crushing the resilience of families and democracy.

This is a painful truth to see and talk about. It will be uncomfortable to have these conversations. Many of us prefer to focus more on positive solutions, because isn't that where real change takes hold? I would argue no.

When *An Inconvenient Truth* came out back in 2006, imagine if Al Gore had stood there with his PowerPoints and talked about the possibilities of solar power, wind power, insulating homes, changing our light bulbs. We would have yawned and walked out saying, *Such nice ideas; too bad they're not catching on.*

Instead he talked about the problem. He put up all those arcane charts about how carbon emissions were soaring, how these gases in the atmosphere trapped heat like a greenhouse, how this created a warming effect that would destabilize natural systems and threaten civilization as we've known it. We walked out of that theater terrified. The scale of the problem blew our minds.

And *because* it blew our minds—*because* the scale of the problem really is that big—people all over the world, by the millions, have been galvanized to develop solutions. That is why all those nice ideas—solar power, wind power—found momentum.

I remember, after that film, hearing people in line at the grocery store talking about climate change. When was the last time you overheard someone at the grocery store talking about financialization? When have you read a magazine article about the problem of "too much finance" and how that's the root of so many crises we face?

We're not talking about the real problem yet. So we're not united. The fight of millions of families to afford food and heat, the fight to save democracy from the assault by the parties of wealth, the struggle of people of color to find security and prosperity, the battle to stave off escalating ecological crises —these could be the streams that feed into a river of a movement that swells beyond resistance into demands for systemic transformation.

These separate battles could become one, if we shared an understanding of the deep system problem that feeds them all—the overgrown, financialized economic system and its insidious processes of wealth extraction, which are the often invisible forces driving so many crises.

We're not connecting the dots yet. We don't hear about the rising number of billionaires and think: opioid crisis, precarious workers barely getting by. As college endowment returns soared not long ago, trustees weren't thinking: local firms shut out by chains, private equity bankrupting companies, Black families losing equity in their homes.[1] When big tech firms' share prices were lofty, we didn't think: post-truth society, corruption of democracy.

We could. As we have seen, these outcomes are symptoms of root causes found in the structures and practices of our capital-centric economy, and in the power that system creates for a wealthy elite.

Where We Begin Is by Talking

We need to talk more about this system crisis. Yes, we do talk about the plutocracy, but not enough about the underlying rules and structures that create it. Not enough about the system logic that leads to financialization and its destabilizing, devastating effects—precarity, monopolies, the capture of government. Not enough about the problem of the machine busy pumping up asset bubbles that burst, CEOs spending trillions on thin air, when the world is on fire.

We need to help each other wrap our heads around the fact that there's too much financial "wealth" in our world; that the extraction this wealth requires is now causing a net loss of strength to society, a loss of resilience, a loss of biodiversity, a loss of families' ability to provide for themselves and rear their young in security.

This will get worse if it is not recognized and dealt with openly.

As we move forward into the Anthropocene—the world where wildness is disappearing, a world of record heat waves and flooding and famine—to continue operating our economy to maximize wealth for the few is the path of madness. What can see us through is the recognition that there is only one living system, the earth; that all of human life is a subsystem of it; and that the only rational economy for the future is one built on the truth that we're all in this together.

Where we begin challenging the current system is by naming wealth supremacy, talking about it. As we track the rise of greenhouse gases, let's also track the rise of financial asset inflation, with frequent analysis and stories of its effects.

Let's help each other get that financialization is more than a collection of obscure charts in academic papers. It's a force in our society—an extractive force of unprecedented power and unimaginable size, the inevitable result of a system built on the myth that no amount of wealth is ever enough.

Let's expose the fact that one-third of GDP is being extracted by the finance industry, make visible the fact that financial assets are five or more times the size of GDP yet still bent on limitless and eternal growth. Let's highlight how this wealth too often is the result of taking from the rest of society. And let's talk about the war on workers as a built-in outcome of this capital-centric system design, this belief that the wealthy matter more than the rest of us.

Recognizing That Financialization and Wealth Supremacy Are Real

Progressives have been locked, for decades, in a cycle of trying to defend the gains of the post-WWII era, aiming to make capitalism less bad even as it's grown more brutal. We've yet to cohere around a radical, positive, united agenda for system change. Neoliberals, by contrast, have remained true to their pure agenda—maximizing gains for the financial elite, while keeping that system free from government restraint—which has brought us our unstable economy of financial overshoot. Since defending this unsustainable system now requires more drastic methods, it is conservatives who have become the revolutionaries.

Deep change, system change, can begin in earnest when society perceives that the problem of financialization and wealth supremacy is real. It is not an ideological shouting match. It's a reality we need to face. Recognizing this is a prelude to the great task ahead—the task of transferring wealth and power from the hands of the few to the control of the many, the task of creating a system designed not to maximize financial wealth but to keep life flourishing.

Cooperatives, worker ownership, public banks, city-controlled water, and the other models of a democratic economy offer a compass point. But in addition to building the positive, we also need to stop the extraction, and that means rooting out and removing capital bias from the design of ownership and corporations and capital markets. At this moment of planetary and societal peril, all economic institutions are needed in the work of serving the public good. The archaic purpose of serving the wealthy few has outlived its day.

To continue its dominance, the centerless mind of capital extraction requires our acceptance of its normality, its legitimacy. We have the power to withhold that legitimacy. We have the power to see and name what's really going on, and to call out the extractive system's disastrous consequences.

Solutions will shift and change. But once we understand the problem of wealth supremacy, we'll be better able to chart our course through the turbulence ahead. There's no guarantee of success. Not even a likelihood of success. But system change doesn't start by asking: Is transformation possible? Instead we ask: Is it *necessary*? It's here we begin.

Wealth Supremacy
Discussion Guide

I HOPE THAT READING *Wealth Supremacy* provided some new insights about our economic system and the potential for systemic change. It may also have raised some questions that might be beneficial to explore in your own circles. These discussion prompts invite you to engage with others in various kinds of dialogue.

One set of questions is about the book's core concepts of wealth supremacy, capital bias, and financialization—how they may be expressed in culture, whether or not you agree with them. The other set of questions is about which models and approaches of building a movement for change might or might not inspire people or catch on.

The cultural context of wealth supremacy, capital bias, and financialization

1. How has capital bias affected you personally?

2. What effects of capital bias have you seen in your community?

3. How do you think our culture and educational systems reflect capital bias?

4. Kelly writes that much of wealth bias is unconscious. Do you agree?

5. To what extent do you think wealth bias is explicit in our society? Where do you see it?

6. What can we learn from other nations and cultures about creating a more equal society?

7. Do you agree with Kelly that "moral capitalism is as impossible as moral racism"?

8. What values in our current economic system should be retained?

9. Many individuals make personal choices not to pursue wealth maximization, yet corporations are expected to do so. Where does that disconnect come from?

10. How much do you think the values of extractive capitalism flow from patriarchal values?

11. Since financialization is such a huge phenomenon, why is it largely missing from the public discourse in the US?

Building a movement

1. Kelly says there isn't yet much of a unified democratic economy movement. Do you agree?

2. Kelly provides many examples of projects aimed at community wealth building and democratic ownership. Do you think these projects can be scaled and become the new norm? What would it take to do that?

3. Kelly suggests a prank of workers running a parallel election for board seats. Can you imagine this at your workplace?

4. Do you think recent changes in the economy as a result of the COVID pandemic (for example, the rise of work-at-home lifestyles) open up more or fewer opportunities for a transition to a more equal society?

5. Do you see opportunities for building a movement in your own community?

6. If you have any money invested, how do you feel about your investing portfolio?

7. Have you ever tried to invest locally?

8. Of the examples Kelly provides of projects challenging extractive capitalism, which ones do you see having the most potential to inspire demoralized workers?

9. Which examples might interest government economic development agencies?

10. How can technological innovation be harnessed to accelerate the transition to a more equal society?

Notes

Chapter 1: Who Will Own the Earth?

1 Ben Ryder Howe, "Wall Street Eyes Billions in the Colorado's Water," *New York Times*, January 3, 2021, *https://nyti.ms/3YU3qXx.*

2 Howe, "Wall Street."

3 Paul Krugman, "Can You Drown Government in an Empty Bathtub?" *New York Times*, September 1, 2022, *https://nyti.ms/3XURfYT.*

4 "The United Nations World Water Development Report," March 19, 2018, *https://www.unwater.org/publications/world-water-development-report-2018.*

5 Shawn Tully, "Water, Water Everywhere," *Fortune*, May 15, 2000, *https://cnn.it/3IYoaYF.*

6 Howe, "Wall Street."

7 Frantz Fanon, *The Wretched of the Earth*, English ed. (New York: Grove Press, 1963, 2021), 6. Citations refer to the 2021 edition.

8 "General Assembly Declares Access to Clean Water and Sanitation Is a Human Right," United Nations, UN News, July 28, 2010, *https://news.un.org/en/story/2010/07/346122.* "Safe and clean drinking water and sanitation is a human right essential to the full enjoyment of human life and all other human rights," the UN declared.

9 Maude Barlow and Tony Clarke, "Who Owns Water?" *The Nation*, August 15, 2002, *https://www.thenation.com/article/archive/who-owns-water/.*

10 Thomas M. Hanna and David A. McDonald, "From Pragmatic to Politicized? The Future of Water Remunicipalization in the United States," *Utilities Policy* 72 (2021).

11 Howe, "Wall Street."

12 Hanna and McDonald, "From Pragmatic to Politicized?"

13 Hadas Thier, "Capital's Muddy Waters," *Jacobin*, June 6, 2022, *https://jacobin.com/2022/06/capitals-muddy-waters.*

14 Hanna and McDonald, "From Pragmatic to Politicized?"; Elizabeth Douglass, "Towns Sell Their Public Water Systems—and Come to Regret It," *Washington Post*, July 8, 2017, *https://wapo.st/3xMWTSp.*

15 Thier, "Capital's Muddy Waters."

16 Hanna and McDonald, "From Pragmatic to Politicized?"

17 Thier, "Capital's Muddy Waters."

Chapter 2: To Form That More Perfect Union

1 Kai Ryssdal, "The U.S. Economy Is Making Us Anxious and Suspicious," June 28, 2016, in NPR's *Marketplace* podcast, *https://www.marketplace.org /2016/06/28/economic-anxiety/*.

2 Between mid-2020 and the end of 2021, a study by the Economic Policy Institute found that 54 percent of inflation was due to increased corporate profits, not to supply shortages. Josh Bivens, "Corporate Profits Have Contributed Disproportionately to Inflation. How Should Policymakers Respond?," Economic Policy Institute, April 21, 2022, *https://www.epi.org/blog/corporate-profits-have -contributed-disproportionately-to-inflation-how-should-policymakers-respond/*.

3 "Introducing Natural Asset Companies (NACs)," accessed September 8, 2022, *https://www.nyse.com/introducing-natural-asset-companies*.

4 $46.46 trillion was the total market capitalization of all US-based publicly listed companies on September 30, 2022. "Total Market Value of the U.S. Stock Market," Siblis Research, accessed January 10, 2023, *https://siblisresearch.com /data/us-stock-market-value/*.

5 Ellen Brown, "Wall Street's Latest Scheme Is Monetizing Nature Itself," Scheer-Post, November 4, 2021, *https://scheerpost.com/2021/11/04/wall-streets-latest -scheme-is-monetizing-nature-itself/*.

6 Elena Shao, "A Biodiversity Crisis Is Affecting Billions," *New York Times*, July 12, 2022.

7 "UN Report: Value of Nature Must Not Be Overridden by Pursuit of Short-Term Profit," UN News, July 11, 2022, *https://news.un.org/en/story/2022 /07/1122322*; Shao, "Biodiversity Crisis."

8 Aldo Leopold, *A Sand County Almanac* (New York: Oxford University Press, 1966), x, 219–220.

9 Nancy McLean, *Democracy in Chains* (New York: Viking Press, 2017), 53. McLean is quoting another source. She wrote: "The paper's owners, as one contemporary noted, took as a given that society separated itself into 'those who ride and those who are the donkeys to be ridden.'"

10 Thomas Piketty, *Capital and Ideology* (Cambridge, MA, and London: Belknap Press of Harvard University Press, 2020), 4.

11 This insight about property is not unique to Piketty. Ellen Meiksins Wood, a historian of comparative political thought, for example, notes that "Western political theory, in all its variations, has been shaped by a distinctive tension between two sources of power, the state and private property," and that "developments in what would be Western Europe . . . gave property, as a distinct locus of power, an unusual degree of autonomy from the state." Wood, *Liberty & Property* (London, New York: Verso, 2012), 4.

12 Eric Hobsbawm, *The Age of Capital: 1848–1875* (New York: Vintage Books, 1996), 31.

13 Antonia Malchik, "The Fox Owns Herself," *On the Commons* (blog), November 11, 2022, *https://antonia.substack.com/p/the-fox-owns-herself*.

14 Claudio Saunt, *Unworthy Republic: The Dispossession of Native Americans and the Road to Indian Territory* (New York: W.W. Norton & Co., 2020), 177, 187.

15 Senator Sheldon Whitehouse, *Captured: The Corporate Infiltration of American Democracy* (New York, London: The New Press, 2017), xvii–xix.

16 Robin Wall Kimmerer, *Braiding Sweetgrass* (Minneapolis: Milkweed Editions, 2013), 17, 58.

17 Kimmerer, *Braiding Sweetgrass*, 366–369.

18 Kimmerer, *Braiding Sweetgrass*, 32.

Chapter 3: Naming Shapes Reality

1 Adrienne Rich, "Twenty-One Love Poems," section IX, *Collected Poems: 1950–2012* (New York, London: W.W. Norton and Co., 2016), 470.

2 Rita Omokha, "Critical Moment," *Vanity Fair*, September 2021, 86–87.

3 Mihee Kim-Kort, "I'm a Scholar of Religion. Here's What I See in the Atlanta Shootings," *New York Times*, March 24, 2021, *https://nyti.ms/3YZLHbo*.

4 Next City, "Economics in Brief: Fees to Small Businesses Are Amazon's Largest Revenue Source, Report Finds," January 7, 2022, *https://nextcity.org/urbanist-news/economics-in-brief-fees-to-small-businesses-are-amazons-largest-revenue*.

5 Deborah Cameron, ed., *The Feminist Critique of Language: A Reader* (London and New York: Routledge, 1990), 12.

6 Claudio Saunt, *Unworthy Republic: The Dispossession of Native Americans ad the Road to Indian Territory* (New York: W.W. Norton & Co., 2020), xiii–xiv.

7 Dale Spender, "Introduction," in *Man Made Language* (London: Routledge & Kegan Paul, 1980), *https://www.marxists.org/reference/subject/philosophy/works/ot/spender.htm*.

8 Cameron, *Feminist Critique*, 1–14, 59–61.

9 These observations are drawn from Marjorie Kelly, *The Divine Right of Capital* (San Francisco: Berrett Koehler, 2001), 30–31. Chapter 2 of that book, "Lords of the Earth: The Principle of Privilege," was an extensive discussion of aristocratic privilege and how it is similar to financial privileges of our day.

10 "Contingent Workforce: Size, Characteristics, Earnings, and Benefits," US Government Accountability Office, April 20, 2015, *https://www.gao.gov/products/gao-15-168r*.

11 Anne Case and Angus Deaton, "Mortality and Morbidity in the 21st Century," Brookings Institution, March 23, 2017, *https://www.brookings.edu/bpea-articles/mortality-and-morbidity-in-the-21st-century/*.

12 Atul Gawande, "The Blight," *New Yorker*, March 23, 2020, 63.

13 Dave Goulson, "The Insect Apocalypse," *Guardian*, July 25, 2021, *https://www .theguardian.com/environment/2021/jul/25/the-insect-apocalypse-our-world-will -grind-to-a-halt-without-them* (excerpt from *Silent Earth: Averting the Insect Apocalypse* [New York: Harper, 2021]).

14 Robert Frank, "The Wealthiest 10% of Americans Own a Record 89% of All U.S. Stocks," CNBC, October 18, 2021, *https://www.cnbc.com/2021/10/18 /the-wealthiest-10percent-of-americans-own-a-record-89percent-of-all-us-stocks .html*.

15 Goulson, "Insect Apocalypse."

16 "Insect apocalypse" is a phrase from Goulson, *Silent Earth*.

17 George Monbiot, "Why Is Life on Earth Still Taking Second Place to Fossil Fuel Companies?" *Guardian Weekly*, August 27, 2021, 47, *https://www.theguardian .com/commentisfree/2021/aug/19/life-earth-second-place-fossil-fuel-climate -breakdown*; Arthur Neslen, "Our Firm Rockhopper Wins £210m Payout After Being Banned from Drilling," *Guardian Weekly*, August 2, 2022, *https://www .theguardian.com/business/2022/aug/24/oil-firm-rockhopper-wins-210m-payout -after-being-banned-from-drilling*.

18 Dean Hand et al., "Annual Impact Investor Survey 2020," Global Impact Investing Network (GIIN), June 11, 2020, xv, *https://thegiin.org/research/publication /impinv-survey-2020/*.

19 Marjorie Kelly, "Holy Grail Found," Musings column, *Business Ethics*, Winter 2004, *https://www.marjoriekelly.org/wp-content/uploads/2021/09/Vol18No 04HolyGrailFound.pdf*.

20 "ESG Assets Rising to $50 Trillion Will Reshape $140.5 Trillion of Global AUM by 2025, Finds Bloomberg Intelligence," July 21, 2021, *https://www .bloomberg.com/company/press/esg-assets-rising-to-50-trillion-will-reshape-140 -5-trillion-of-global-aum-by-2025-finds-bloomberg-intelligence/*.

21 Tim Stobierski, "15 Eye-Opening Corporate Social Responsibility Statistics," Harvard Business School Online, June 15, 2021, *https://online.hbs.edu/blog /post/corporate-social-responsibility-statistics*.

22 Cam Simpson, Akshat Rathi, and Saijel Kishan, "The ESG Mirage," December 10, 2021, in Bloomberg's *The Big Take* podcast, *https://www.bloomberg.com /news/audio/2021-12-10/the-esg-mirage-podcast*.

23 Simpson et al., "The ESG Mirage."

24 George Lakoff, *Don't Think of an Elephant* (White River Junction, Vermont: Chelsea Green Publishing, 2004).

25 Andrew Ross Sorkin et al., "BlackRock Seeks to Defend Its Reputation Over E.S.G. Fight," *New York Times*, September 8, 2022, *https://nyti.ms/3KywDD4*; Kenneth Vogel, "The Hidden Hand Guiding Conservative Causes," *New York Times*, October 13, 2022, *https://nyti.ms/3kviL1s*.

26 Duncan Austin, "Market-Led Sustainabilty Is a 'Fix That Fails,'" Both Brains Required, October 25, 2021, *https://bothbrainsrequired.com/*.

27 Tariq Fancy, "The Secret Diary of a 'Sustainable Investor,'" Medium, August 20, 2021, *https://medium.com/@sosofancy/the-secret-diary-of-a-sustainable-investor-part-1-70b6987fa139*.

28 Anand Giridharadas, *Winners Take All* (New York: Vintage Books/A Division of Penguin Random House, 2018), 6–8.

29 Edgar Villanueva, *Decolonizing Wealth: Indigenous Wisdom to Heal Divides and Restore Balance* (San Francisco: Berrett-Koehler Publishers, 2018), 1–3, 5.

30 Ralph Thurm, "The Big Sustainability Illusion—Finding a Maturation Pathway for Regeneration & Thriving," r3.0, March 2021, *https://www.r3-0.org/wp-content/uploads/2021/04/Opinion-Paper-1-Ralph-Thurm-The-Big-Sustainability-Illusion-March-2021.pdf*.

31 Michael L. Barnett et al., "Reorient the Business Case for Corporate Sustainability," *Stanford Social Innovation Review* (Summer 2021).

32 Robert Kuttner, "The Agony of Social Democratic Europe," *The American Prospect*, August 4, 2021, *https://prospect.org/world/agony-social-democratic-europe-trans-atlantic-left/*.

33 Thomas M. Hanna, "The Supreme Court Is Gutting the Regulatory State. Let's Look at Our Other Options," *In These Times*, July 27, 2022, *https://inthesetimes.com/article/supreme-court-regulatory-state-environmental-protection-agency-climate-change*.

34 Elisabeth Asbrink, "Sweden Is Becoming Unbearable," *New York Times*, September 20, 2022, *https://nyti.ms/3KxtnYk*.

35 Kuttner, "Agony."

36 "Day One Message to Staff from Secretary of the United States Treasury Janet L. Yellen," press release, US Department of the Treasury, January 26, 2021, *https://home.treasury.gov/news/press-releases/jy0003*.

37 Robert Kuttner, "Capitalism vs. Liberty," *The American Prospect*, November/December 2021, 47, *https://prospect.org/politics/capitalism-vs-liberty/*.

38 George Monbiot, "This Heatwave Has Eviscerated the Idea That Small Changes Can Tackle Extreme Weather," *Guardian*, July 1, 2022, *https://www.theguardian.com/commentisfree/2022/jul/18/heatwave-extreme-weather-uk-climate-crisis*.

39 President Joseph Biden, "Remarks by President Biden on the Economy," The White House, September 16, 2021, *https://www.whitehouse.gov/briefing-room/speeches-remarks/2021/09/16/remarks-by-president-biden-on-the-economy-4/*.

40 Michael Kazin, *What It Took to Win: A History of the Democratic Party* (New York: Farrar, Straus and Giroux, 2022).

Chapter 4: Calling Out the Deep Forces at Work

1 The "white farmers" were cited often in the news; the lawsuits were brought by the America First Legal (AFL) Foundation, touted May 3, 2021, on Fox News by former White House senior advisor Stephen Miller, the AFL's president; the group was formed in May 2021 to sue the Biden administration on behalf

of white people. The group's six other board members include at least four
Trump administration veterans. Ray Hartmann, "This Former Trump Aide
Just Launched a New Group—and It's Both Pathetic and Shady as Hell," Raw
Story, May 3, 2021, https://www.rawstory.com/america-first-legal-foundation/.
Also see Josh Gerstein and Ximena Bustillo, "Historic Debt Relief for Minority
Farmers Faces Legal Juggernaut," Politico, August 3, 2021, https://politi.co
/3YNZJCx.

2   Hartmann, "Former Trump Aide"; Gerstein and Bustillo, "Historic Debt Relief."

3   Alan Rappeport, "Banks Fight $4 Billion Debt Relief for Black Farmers," New
York Times, May 19, 2021, https://nyti.ms/3ZgbcKR.

4   Rappeport, "Banks."

5   Autodidact 17, "Dr. Martin Luther King Jr: 'I Fear I Am Integrating My People
into a Burning House,'" New York Amsterdam News, January 12, 2017, https://
amsterdamnews.com/news/2017/01/12/dr-martin-luther-king-jr-i-fear-i-am
-integrating-m/.

6   Chuck Quirmbach, "Wisconsin Is Again Leading the Nation in Farm Bank-
ruptcies," NPR's Morning Edition, September 10, 2019, https://n.pr/2m5aina.

7   Katy Milani and Stacy Mitchell, "Senate Testimony: Concentration Is at the
Root of Rural Distress," Institute for Local Self-Reliance, April 27, 2021,
https://ilsr.org/stacy-mitchells-senate-testimony-on-state-of-rural-economy/.

8   The more recent legislation passed was the Inflation Reduction Act (IRA),
which created two funds, one with $3.1 billion for loan adjustments for farm-
ers who are facing financial distress and hold Farm Service Agency loans. The
USDA has distributed $800 million from this fund in loan payments and debt
clearance to roughly thirteen thousand farmers; no breakdown on race could be
found. The other IRA fund provides $2.2 billion for those who faced past dis-
crimination from the USDA. The public comment period on that fund ended
November 14, 2022; as of late January 2023, there was no indication any of that
funding had been distributed. The original lawsuit over the American Rescue
Plan (ARP) provision to assist socially disadvantaged farmers—Boyd et al. v.
United States of America—was ongoing as of early February 2023. Leah Doug-
las, "Analysis: Biden Debt Relief Plan Disappoints Black Farmers for Avoiding
Race," Reuters, August 17, 2022, https://reut.rs/3Ireww7; Leah Douglas,
"Minority Farmers Sue U.S. Government Over Repealed Debt Relief Program,"
Reuters, October 12, 2022, https://reut.rs/3EAfO6F; April Simpson, "Can You
Tackle Systemic Racism Without Confronting Race?" Center for Public Integ-
rity, October 21, 2022, https://publicintegrity.org/labor/can-you-tackle-system-
ic-racism-without-confronting-race/; Leah Douglas, "U.S. Farmers Receive Nearly
$800 Mln. in Loan Relief from Agriculture Agency," Reuters, October 18, 2022,
https://reut.rs/3IPMAn1; "USDA Seeking Public Comment on a New Provision to Provide Assistance to Agricultural Producers Who Have Experienced
Discrimination," US Department of Agriculture, October 13, 2022, https://

www.usda.gov/media/press-releases/2022/10/13/usda-seeking-public-comment
-new-provision-provide-assistance; Adam Minter, "Biden Is Still Failing America's
Black Farmers," *Washington Post*, December 1, 2022, https://wapo.st/3kmFj4u.

9 Craig Hall, "How the Decline in Community Banks Has Hurt U.S. Entrepre-
neurship," *Barron's*, May 18, 2019, https://www.barrons.com/articles/how-the
-decline-in-community-banks-has-hurt-u-s-entrepreneurship-51558184413; William R. Emmons, "Slow, Steady Decline in the Number of U.S. Banks Continues," *On the Economy* blog, Federal Reserve Bank of St. Louis, December 9,
2021, https://www.stlouisfed.org/on-the-economy/2021/december/steady-decline
-number-us-banks.

10 S&P Dow Jones Indices, through December 30, 2021.

Part II: The Myths of Wealth Supremacy

1 Robin DiAngelo, "Whiteness in Racial Dialogue: A Discourse Analysis," PhD
diss., University of Washington, 2004, 1–5.

2 T. S. Eliot, "Tradition and the Individual Talent," *The Egoist* 6, nos. 4 and 5
(September and December, 1919).

3 Quoted in Isaiah David Wexler, "Burke's Concept of Property (England)," PhD
diss., Fordham University, 1983, 8–9, 37, 62–64. Other quotes in Don Herzog,
Poisoning the Minds of the Lower Orders (Princeton, NJ: Princeton University
Press, 1998), 504, 154.

4 Herzog, *Poisoning*, 182–183, 245.

Chapter 5: No Amount of Wealth Is Ever Enough

1 Sara Morrison, "MacKenzie Scott Gives Away Billions, Again," Vox, June 15,
2021, https://www.vox.com/recode/2021/6/15/22535094/mackenzie-scott
-charity-donations-amazon.

2 Tara Frances Chan, "Communist China Has 104 Billionaires Leading the
Country while Xi Jinping Promises to Lift Millions Out of Poverty," *Business
Insider*, March 2, 2018, https://www.businessinsider.in/Communist-China-has
-104-billionaires-leading-the-country-while-Xi-Jinping-promises-to-lift-millions-out
-of-poverty/articleshow/63141726.cms.

3 Justin Harper, "Beijing Now Has More Billionaires Than Any City," BBC News,
April 8, 2021, https://bbc.in/3Ss9d3P.

4 Allison Morrow, "The World's 500 Richest People Became $1 Trillion Richer
Last Year," CNN Business, January 4, 2022, https://cnn.it/3Ss75JB.

5 In 1773, the year after the share price doubled, the bubble burst as "plunder and
famine in Bengal led to massive shortfalls in expected land revenues." The East
India Company had to be saved by a mega-bailout, "the first example of a nation
state extracting, as its price for saving a failing corporation, the right to regulate
and severely rein it in." William Dalrymple, *The Anarchy* (New York, London:
Bloomsbury Publishing, 2019), xxiv–xxxv.

6   The "scramble for Africa" occurred during the period of the New Imperialism, 1881–1914.

7   For Rodney, see, for example: "For the most part, the nations of Africa fall into the group of exploited countries inside the capitalist/imperialist system." Walter Rodney, *How Europe Underdeveloped Africa* (Brooklyn and London: Verso Books, 2018), 29–30.

8   Duncan Bell, *Dreamworlds of Race: Empire and the Utopian Destiny of Anglo-America* (Princeton and Oxford, Princeton University Press, 2020), 1, footnote 2.

9   Ben Johnson, "Cecil Rhodes," Historic UK, accessed November 5, 2021, *https:// www.historic-uk.com/HistoryUK/HistoryofEngland/Cecil-Rhodes/*; Stan Winer, "How Diamonds Destroyed a People," George Washington University: History News Network, April 20, 2015, *https://historynewsnetwork.org/article/158987*; Selected Diamond website, accessed October 28, 2021, *https://www.selected diamond.com/single-post/2017/12/26/de-beers-group*. De Beers Diamonds' 2022 revenue from "De Beers 2022 Revenues Rise 18% to $6.6 Billion," *Diamond World*, February 24, 2023; Bell, *Dreamworlds of Race*, 141.

10 Bell, *Dreamworlds of Race*, 131.

11 The ratio of CEO to typical worker compensation in 2020 was 351:1 under the realized measure of CEO pay, up from 21:1 in 1965. Lawrence Mishel and Jori Kandra, "CEO Pay Has Skyrocketed 1,322% Since 1978," Economic Policy Institute, August 10, 2021, *https://www.epi.org/publication/ceo-pay-in-2020/*.

12 Abha Bhattarai, "Rents Are Up More Than 30 Percent in Some Cities, Forcing Millions to Find Another Place to Live," *Washington Post*, January 30, 2022, *https://wapo.st/3KuO1bL*.

13 The endowment of Washington University in St. Louis realized a 65 percent gain in 2021. The median return at US colleges for the 2021 fiscal year was 27 percent, wrote Mike Scutari, "University Endowments Have Grown Dramatically. How Should Officials Allocate the Earnings?," Inside Philanthropy, January 13, 2022, *https://www.insidephilanthropy.com/home/2022/1/13/university-endowments -have-grown-dramatically-how-should-officials-allocate-the-earnings*.

14 Austan Goolsbee, "Big Companies Are Starting to Swallow the World," *New York Times*, September 30, 2020, *https://nyti.ms/3KueGp3*.

15 "Cecil Rhodes, Apartheid Architect, Born 07.05.1853," accessed December 7, 2021, *https://aaregistry.org/story/cecil-rhodes-born/*; Johnson, "Cecil Rhodes."

16 Stan Winer, "How Diamonds Destroyed a People," George Washington University: History News Network, April 20, 2015, *https://historynewsnetwork.org /article/158987*.

17 Bell, *Dreamworlds of Race*, 35.

18 Marin Independent Journal, "Smith & Hawken to Close; Going-Out-of-Business Sales Started," *San Jose Mercury News*, July 9, 2009, *https://www.mercurynews.com /2009/07/09/smith-hawken-to-close-going-out-of-business-sales-started-thursday/*.

19 I explored this fact at length in *The Divine Right of Capital* (San Francisco: Berrett-Koehler, 2001). See chapter 4 on corporate governance.

20 SCORE, "Family-Owned Businesses Create 78% of New U.S. Jobs and Employ 60% of the Workforce," PR Newswire, March 14, 2018, *https://www.prnews wire.com/news-releases/family-owned-businesses-create-78-of-new-us-jobs-and -employ-60-of-the-workforce-300613665.html*.

21 Sarah Stranahan and Marjorie Kelly, "Mission-Led Employee-Owned Firms: The Best of the Best," Fifty by Fifty, April 23, 2019, *https://www.fiftybyfifty. org/2019/04/mission-led-employee-owned-firms-the-best-of-the-best-2/*.

Chapter 6: Expanding Wealth Is a Sacred Obligation

1 Paul Kiel et al., "America's Highest Earners and Their Taxes Revealed," ProPublica, April 13, 2022, *https://projects.propublica.org/americas-highest -incomes-and-taxes-revealed/*.

2 Ross Kerber, "U.S. CEO Pay Soars 31% on Stock and Cash Awards, Study Finds," Reuters, April 18, 2022, *https://reut.rs/3m0EGOz*; Kiel et al, "America's Highest Earners."

3 I am indebted for the phrase "asset management capitalism" to labor educator Ericka Wills, "Miners vs. Wall Street: Strikes in the Era of Asset Management Capitalism," *Nonprofit Quarterly*, March 16, 2022, *https://nonprofitquarterly.org /miners-wall-street-and-supercomputers-strikes-in-the-era-of-asset-management -capitalism/*.

4 Figures from 2021, sourced from *https://www.icifactbook.org/pdf/2022_fact- book.pdf*; *https://crsreports.congress.gov/product/pdf/IF/IF12117/2*; *https:// s24.q4cdn.com/856567660/files/doc_financials/2022/ar/2022-Proxy-Statement _vF.pdf*; *https://www.thinkingaheadinstitute.org/news/article/top-500-asset -managers-reach-new-us131-trillion-record/*.

5 Edward Said, *Culture and Imperialism* (London: Chatto & Windus, 1993), 15, 82.

6 Cited by Chris Hunt, "Living King's Dreams or His Nightmares," *Portland Press Herald*, January 18, 2021, *https://www.une.edu/news/2021/living-kings-dreams -or-his-nightmares*.

7 John Stuart Mill, *Principles of Political Economy*, vol. 3, ed. J. M. Robinson (Toronto: University of Toronto Press, 1965), 693. Cited by Said, *Culture and Imperialism*, 59.

8 Said, *Culture and Imperialism*, 81.

9 Said, *Culture and Imperialism*, 59, 81.

10 Gloria Oladipo, "How Chris Smalls Defied the Might of Amazon to Form a Union," *Guardian Weekly*, April 15, 2022, 33, *https://www.theguardian.com/us -news/2022/apr/10/chris-smalls-amazon-union-staten-island*.

11 Sofi Thanhauser, "The Great Stitch-Up: How the US Exploited the Garment Industry in Honduras," *Guardian*, February 4, 2022, *https://www.theguardian .com/news/2022/jan/25/behind-the-label-how-the-us-stitched-up-the-honduras -garment-industry*.

12 A Knight Foundation study looked at a sample representing $82.24 trillion AUM, finding that only 1.4 percent of total US AUM is managed by diverse (women- and minority-owned) firms, as of September 2021. Knight Foundation, "Knight Diversity of Asset Managers Research Series: Industry," December 7, 2021, https://knightfoundation.org/reports/knight-diversity-of-asset -managers-research-series-industry/.

13 Max M. Schanzenbach and Robert H. Sitkoff, "Reconciling Fiduciary Duty and Social Conscience: The Law and Economics of ESG Investing by a Trustee," *Stanford Law Review* 72 (February 2020): 381–382.

14 Rajaie Batniji, a physician and cofounder of Collective Health, recounted this anecdote to Noam Scheiber, "The Private Sector Can't Pay for Everything," *New York Times*, October 11, 2020, https://nyti.ms/3Ss1XVQ.

15 Schanzenbach and Sitkoff, "Reconciling."

16 State Street assets under custody/administration were $43.7 trillion at year-end 2021; assets under management were $4.1 trillion. Funds Europe, "State Street Global Advisors AUM Hits $4.1 Trillion in Q4; CEO Confirms Planned Retirement," January 20, 2022, https://www.funds-europe.com/news/state-street -global-advisors-aum-hits-41-trillion-in-q4-ceo-confirms-planned-retirement.

17 Cyrus Taraporevala and Benjamin Colton, "The Just Interview: State Street Global Advisors' CEO and Head of Asset Stewardship Talk Proxy Season, the State of Energy Amid Ukraine War, and the Future of ESG," Just Capital email newsletter from State Street, March 10, 2022, https://justcapital.com/news /state-street-global-advisors-ceo-taraporevala-and-asset-stewardship-head-colton-on -esg-2022-proxy-voting-and-ukraine-war/.

18 Freedom of association and collective bargaining is a fundamental human right proclaimed in Article 23 of the Universal Declaration of Human Rights adopted by the United National General Assembly in 1948.

19 Isaiah David Wexler, "Burke's Concept of Property," PhD diss., Fordham University, 1983, 8–9, 31, 35, 49.

20 The description of paupers drawing wagons is from an 1830 lecture by William Cobbett, *Eleven Lectures on the French and Belgian Revolutions, and English Boroughmongering.* "People have been drawing wagons, chained or harnessed together like beasts of burden. In Nottinghamshire, I met twenty men harnessed in this way, and in Sussex, in Hertfordshire, and in Hampshire, it has been common." Cited by Don Herzog, *Poisoning the Minds of the Lower Orders* (Princeton, NJ: Princeton University Press, 1998), 198–199.

21 Sir William Blackstone, *Commentaries on the Laws of England in Four Books* (Philadelphia: J.B. Lippincott Co., 1893), https://oll.libertyfund.org/page /blackstone-on-property-1753.

22 See, for example, "Universal Ownership: Exploring Opportunities and Challenges," conference report, St. Mary's College of California, Center for the Study of Fiduciary Capitalism, April 10–11, 2006, https://community-wealth.org

/sites/clone.community-wealth.org/files/downloads/report-hawley-williams.pdf.
The report noted that by 2005, the one hundred largest institutions and managers owned 52 percent of all publicly traded equity. Today, institutions own about 80 percent of the public equity market. The quote from Hiro Mizuno is from "Universal Owners," September 10, 2021, in *ImpactAlpha, https://impactalpha .com/universal-owners/.*

23 Margaret Blair and Lynn Stout, "A Team Production Theory of Corporate Law," *Virginia Law Review* 85, no. 2 (March 1999), *http://ssrn.com/abstract=425500.*

24 Lynn Stout, "The Shareholder Value Myth," Harvard Law School Forum on Corporate Governance, June 26, 2012, *https://corpgov.law.harvard.edu/2012 /06/26/the-shareholder-value-myth/.*

25 A valuable review of the concept of intergenerational equity is found in Arjya Majumdar, "The Fiduciary Responsibility of Directors to Preserve Intergenerational Equity," *Journal of Business Ethics* (2017): 1–12.

26 Joakim Sandberg, "(Re)Interpreting Fiduciary Duty to Justify Socially Responsible Investment for Pension Funds," *Corporate Governance* 21, no. 5 (2013), *https://philpapers.org/rec/SANRFD.*

27 "ESG: The EU's Agenda for 2022—What You Need to Know," WilmerHale (international law firm) Client Alerts, February 10, 2022, *https://www.wilmer hale.com/en/insights/client-alerts/02102022-esg-the-eu-agenda-for-2022-what -you-need-to-know.*

28 "Universal Ownership."

29 Annual Reports and Financial Statements, BlueHub Capital, accessed May 4, 2022. "BlueHub Capital's SUN Initiative Reaches 10-Year Milestone Helping Homeowners in Foreclosure, Stabilizing Neighborhoods," PR Newswire, January 21, 2020, *https://www.prnewswire.com/news-releases/bluehub-capitals-sun -initiative-reaches-10-year-milestone-helping-homeowners-in-foreclosure-stabilizing -neighborhoods-300990357.html.*

30 "BlueHub Capital's SUN Initiative."

31 "Homeowners Join Class Action Lawsuit Against Roxbury Based BlueHub Alleging Predatory Lending Practices," GBH News, February 18, 2020, *https:// www.wgbh.org/news/local-news/2020/02/18/homeowners-join-class-action-lawsuit -against-roxbury-based-bluehub-capital-alleging-predatory-lending-practices.* In author dialogue and email correspondence in 2022 with Leslie Christian of NorthStar Asset Management, she expressed concern that BlueHub's profits from the SUN initiative were in her estimation too high for the mission it was pursuing.

Chapter 7: The Unseen Underside of Wealth

1 Conrad de Aenlle, "The Markets Have Prospered. Why Are So Many People Worried?," *New York Times,* July 9, 2021, *https://nyti.ms/3KDTCww.*

2 Tommy Wilkes, "Emerging Markets Drive Global Debt to Record $303 Trillion—IIF," Reuters, February 23, 2022, *https://reut.rs/3ktjcta.*

3   Federal Reserve, "Domestic Financial Sectors; Total Financial Assets, Level/ (Gross Domestic Product*1000)," second quarter 2022, FRED Economic Data, St. Louis Federal Reserve, accessed November 19, 2022, *https://fred.stlouisfed .org/graph/?g=WAtK*.

4   Jean-Louise Arcand, Enrico Berkes, and Ugo Panizza, "Too Much Finance?," International Monetary Fund Working Paper, June 2012, *https://www.imf.org /external/pubs/ft/wp/2012/wp12161.pdf*. Also see, for example, Ratna Sahay, Martin Čihák, and Papa N'Diaye, "How Much Finance Is Too Much: Stability, Growth & Emerging Markets," IMF Blog, May 5, 2015, *https://www.imf.org /en/Blogs/Articles/2015/05/04/how-much-finance-is-too-much-stability-growth -emerging-markets#.ZAjEpsxsTO4.link*.

5   Dirk Bezemer, Michael Hudson, and Howard Reed, "Exploring the Capital Gains Economy: The Case of the UK," 2022 unpublished working paper commissioned by the Democracy Collaborative.

6   Bezemer et al., "Exploring."

7   Kevin Phillips, *American Theocracy* (New York: Viking Penguin, 2006), 268.

8   Economist Dirk Bezemer reported there was roughly $235 trillion in global debt and $105 trillion in stock market capitalization as of 2021, citing Statista.com as the source; author email correspondence with Bezemer, January 25, 2023.

9   Atif R. Mian, Ludwig Straub, and Amir Sufi, "The Saving Glut of the Rich," National Bureau of Economic Research Working Paper No. 26941, April 2020, *https://www.nber.org/papers/w26941*. Cited in Delilah Rothenberg, Raphaele Chappe, and Amanda Feldman, "ESG 2.0: Measuring and Managing Investor Risks Beyond the Enterprise-Level," April 6, 2021, *https://ssrn.com/abstract =3820316*.

10 See chapter 11 for a fuller description of financialization and full endnotes on sources. For International Monetary Fund research, see, for example, Arcand et al., "Too Much Finance?" and Sahay et al., "How Much Finance." Other sources include Rothenberg et al., "ESG 2.0" and Nicholas Shaxson, *The Finance Curse* (New York: Grove Press, 2019).

11 Thomas Piketty, *Capital in the Twenty-First Century* (Cambridge and London: Belknap Press, 2014).

12 Bezemer et al., "Exploring."

13 Jayati Ghosh, "Control the Vampire Companies: Skyrocketing Corporate Profits Spur Global Inequalities," *Dollars & Sense* (July/August 2022); Nabil Ahmed et al., "Inequality Kills," Oxfam International, January 17, 2022, *https://www .oxfam.org/en/research/inequality-kills*.

Chapter 8: Workers Are Not Members of the Corporation

1   Quoted by Tyler Stovall, "The Untold History of Freedom," *The Nation*, April 5/ 12, 2021, *https://www.thenation.com/article/society/annelien-de-dijn-freedom -history/*.

2 Marjorie Kelly et al., *Worker Equity in Food and Agriculture: Practices at the 100 Largest and Most Influential U.S. Companies* (Boston: Tellus Institute, 2012).

3 Elise Gould and Jori Kandra, "State of Working America 2021: Measuring Wages in the Pandemic Market," Economic Policy Institute, April 27, 2022, *https://epi.org/247140*.

4 To equate profit with shareholder income is a simplification. Profits are not paid out directly to shareholders. However, conceptually, profit (EBITDA) is divided into earnings per share (a measure of profit per share), and earnings per share is a common measure of company share value. As profits/earnings rise, shareholders pocket the corresponding rise in company value. In fact, each dollar of profit tends to be multiplied in the stock market by the magic of the multiple, such that if the price-to-earnings ratio is, say, 26, each dollar of profit becomes $26 in stock value. Thus shareholders get far *more* than profit; they get earnings per share multiplied by the P/E ratio. I discuss this at greater length in *The Divine Right of Capital*, chapter 2, and *Owning Our Future*, chapter 3.

5 James Manyika et al., "A New Look at How Corporations Impact the Economy and Households," discussion paper, McKinsey Global Institute, May 31, 2021, *https://mck.co/3yqX4mN*.

6 James Galbraith, "Taming Predatory Capitalism," *The Nation*, March 30, 2006.

7 Andrea Hsu, "Starbucks Says Employees Getting New Benefits, but Not at Stores That Are Unionizing," National Public Radio, May 3, 2022, *https://n.pr /428dnma*.

8 US Bureau of Labor Statistics, Labor Force Statistics from the Current Population Survey, April 2022, *https://www.bls.gov/cps/*.

9 Labor Force Participation Rate, FRED Economic Data, St. Louis Federal Reserve, *https://fred.stlouisfed.org/series/CIVPART*. One reason for the decline in LFPR is the aging of the baby boomers, who started reaching age sixty-two, the earliest retirement age, in 2008. Another reason is "missing workers," those who would be working if the employment situation were better. Still another reason is the millions of former workers who, giving up on finding work, applied for and received disability.

10 "How the Government Measures Unemployment," US Bureau of Labor Statistics, Labor Force Statistics from the Current Population Survey, *https://www .bls.gov/cps/cps_htgm.htm*.

11 "Contingent Workforce: Size, Characteristics, Earnings, and Benefits," US Government Accountability Office, April 20, 2015, *https://www.gao.gov/products /gao-15-168r*.

12 Lauren Weber, "The End of Employees," *Wall Street Journal*, February 2, 2017, *https://on.wsj.com/3SXKXXL*.

13 Weber, "The End."

14 CAGE Research Centre, "Unemployment Substantially Increases Domestic Violence, New Study Finds," University of Warwick (Coventry, UK), October 5,

2021, *https://warwick.ac.uk/fac/soc/economics/research/centres/cage/ news/05-10-21-unemployment_substantially_increases_domestic_violence_new_study_finds/*; Beth Braverman, "5 Ways the Economy Is Undermining Marriage," *Fiscal Times*, March 27, 2015, *https://www.thefiscaltimes. com/2015/03/27/5-Ways-Economy-Undermining-Marriage*; Arthur Goldsmith and Timothy Diette, "Exploring the Link Between Unemployment and Mental Health Outcomes," *SES Indicator*, American Psychological Association (April 2012), *https://www.apa.org/pi/ses/resources/indicator/2012/04/unemployment*. "Unemployment in California," KidsData, accessed March 8, 2023, *https://www .kidsdata.org/topic/43/unemployment/summary*.

15 In 1979, the Conservative government in the UK abolished controls on the London Stock Exchange, triggering what for some was an economic and financial revival of the UK. A new culture of rates and bonuses was established, rewarding profit making and short-term thinking. Earnings for finance became colossal, and a new dog-eat-dog environment set in. Jamie Robertson, "How the Big Bang Changed the City of London For Ever," BBC News, October 27, 2016, *https://www.bbc.com/news/business-37751599*.

16 The Dow Jones Industrial Average was on a largely downward slope from 1965 to 1982, close to two decades. Historical data is inflation-adjusted using the headline CPI. "Dow Jones – DJIA – 100 Year Historical Chart," Macrotrends, accessed March 8, 2023, *https://www.macrotrends.net/1319/dow-jones-100 -year-historical-chart*.

17 Richard Hernandez, "The Fall of Employment in the Manufacturing Sector," *Monthly Labor Review*, US Bureau of Labor Statistics, August 2018, *https:// www.bls.gov/opub/mlr/2018/beyond-bls/the-fall-of-employment-in-the -manufacturing-sector.htm*.

18 From 1980 to 2021, labor's share of income fell from close to 50 percent down to 43.9 percent, a drop of roughly 12 percent. "Shares of Gross Domestic Income: Compensation of Employees, Paid: Wage and Salary Accruals: Disbursements: To Persons," FRED Economic Data, St. Louis Federal Reserve, accessed March 8, 2023, *https://fred.stlouisfed.org/series/W270RE1A156NBEA*.

19 David Gelles, "Jack Welch and the Rise of C.E.O.s Behaving Badly," *New York Times*, May 22, 2022, *https://nyti.ms/3YBVt8a*; adapted from Gelles's book on Welch, *The Man Who Broke Capitalism* (New York: Simon & Schuster, 2022).

20 Adam Hochschild, "Who's to Blame?" review of *American Made: What Happens to People When Work Disappears*, by Farah Stockman, *New York Review of Books*, May 12, 2022, *https://www.nybooks.com/articles/2022/05/12/wildland -the-making-of-americas-fury-osnos-hochschild/*.

Chapter 9: Ecological and Societal Damages Are Not Real

1 Eileen Applebaum and Rosemary Batt, *Private Equity at Work: When Wall Street Manages Main Street* (New York: Russell Sage Foundation, 2014),

3; Ben Protess and Michael Corkery, "Just How Much Do the Top Private Equity Earners Make?," *New York Times*, December 10, 2016, *https://nyti.ms /3J54C3m*. The statistic of more than half of corporate defaults in the pandemic being due to private equity is from David Dayen, "Cut Off Private Equity's Money Spigot," *American Prospect*, August 2022, 21, *https://prospect.org /economy/cut-off-private-equitys-money-spigot/*.

2 Hannah Levintova, "The Smash-and-Grab Economy," *Mother Jones*, May/ June 2022, *https://www.motherjones.com/politics/2022/05/private-equity -buyout-kkr-houdaille/*; "McKinsey's Private Markets Annual Review," from March 24, 2022, reported that private capital markets' AUM reached $9.8 trillion in July 2021; see *https://mck.co/3L9hisW*.

3 Global Fossil Fuel Divestment Commitments Database, accessed July 28, 2022, *https://divestmentdatabase.org/*.

4 Bill McKibben, "This Movement Is Taking Money Away From Fossil Fuels, and It's Working," *New York Times*, October 26, 2021, *https://nyti.ms/3L9htEr*.

5 Hiroko Tabuchi, "Private Equity Funds, Sensing Profit in Tumult, Are Propping Up Oil," *New York Times*, October 13, 2021, *https://nyti.ms/3l0vdqq*.

6 Hiroko Tabuchi, "Oil Giants Sell Dirty Wells to Buyers with Looser Climate Goals, Study Finds," *New York Times*, May 10, 2022, *https://nyti.ms/3Yw7Wu7*.

7 Alyssa Giachino, "KKR's Fracking Footprint Expands as KKR's Contango Buys Drilling Assets Sold by ConocoPhillips," Private Equity Stakeholder Project, July 15, 2021, *https://pestakeholder.org/news/ kkrs-fracking-footprint-expands-buys-drilling-assets-sold-by-conocophillips/*.

8 Nina Lakhani, "Private Equity's Dirty Dozen: The 12 US Firms Funding Dirty Energy Projects," *Guardian*, February 15, 2022, *https://www.theguardian.com/ environment/2022/feb/15/us-private-equity-firms-funding-dirty-energy-projects*; Nina Lakhani, "US Supreme Court Rejects Dakota Access Pipeline Appeal," *Guardian*, February 22, 2022, *https://www.theguardian.com/us-news/2022 /feb/22/us-supreme-court-dakota-access-pipeline*; "The Dakota Access Pipeline Is Operating Without a Permit," Indian Country Today, March 23, 2022, *https:// ictnews.org/newscasts/03-23-2022*.

9 Alyssa Giachino and Riddhi Mehta-Neugebauer, "Private Equity Propels the Climate Crisis," Private Equity Stakeholder Project, October 2021, *https:// pestakeholder.org/reports/private-equity-propels-the-climate-crisis-the-risks-of-a -shadowy-industrys-massive-exposure-to-oil-gas-and-coal/*.

10 "UN Climate Report: It's 'Now or Never' to Limit Global Warming to 1.5 Degrees," United Nations, April 4, 2022, *https://news.un.org/en/story/2022 /04/1115452*.

11 Levintova, "Smash-and-Grab."

12 2020 Annual Tax Return, Form 990-PF, Ford Foundation, accessed March 8, 2023, *https://www.fordfoundation.org/media/6873/ford-fdn-2020-form -990-pf.pdf*.

13 Alicia McElhaney, "Desperate for Access to Flagship Funds, Allocators Struggle to Say No to GPs," *Institutional Investor*, May 24, 2022, *https://www.institutionalinvestor.com/article/b1y5p46gpt39k7/Desperate-for-Access-to-Flagship-Funds-Allocators-Struggle-to-Say-No-to-GPs*.

14 John Bowman, executive vice president of CAIA Association, which advocates for general and limited partners, quoted in McElhaney, "Desperate."

15 James Comtois, "Harvard Endowment Gains 33.6%, Rises to $53.2 Billion," *Pensions & Investments*, October 14, 2021, *https://www.pionline.com/endowments-and-foundations/harvard-endowment-gains-336-rises-532-billion*.

16 Kia Kokalitcheva, *Axios Pro Rata* email newsletter, July 21, 2022.

17 Kokalitcheva, *Axios Pro Rata*.

18 "According to the American Investment Council, in the decade preceding September 2020, private equity funds generated a 14.2% median annualized return compared to an annualized return of 13.7% for the S&P 500." Julian Gary, "Does Private Equity Outperform Public Markets?" *Economics Review at New York University*, June 10, 2022.

19 Jennifer Louis, CPA, "What Is Materiality? The AICPA Definition of Materiality Changes," Becker Professional Education, accessed March 8, 2023, *https://www.becker.com/blog/accounting/aicpa-adopts-new-definition-of-materiality*.

20 Private Equity Firms database, Private Equity Info, accessed July 29, 2022, *https://www.privateequityinfo.com/product-details/private_equity_firms*.

21 Heather Vogell, "When Private Equity Becomes Your Landlord," ProPublica, February 7, 2022, *https://www.propublica.org/article/when-private-equity-becomes-your-landlord*.

22 Vogell, "Private Equity."

23 Hannah Levintova, "Flipped Off," *Mother Jones*, May/June 2022, 25, *https://www.motherjones.com/politics/2022/05/private-equity-brooklyn-park-slope-greenbrook-nw1-mcnam-schumer/*.

24 McKay Coppins, "The Men Who Are Killing America's Newspapers," *Atlantic*, November 2021; Noah Lanard and Abigail Weinberg, "Sold Out," *Mother Jones*, May/June 2022, *https://www.motherjones.com/politics/2022/05/alden-global-capital-hedge-fund-private-equity-pottstown-journal/*.

25 Elizabeth Williamson, "How the Sandy Hook Families Emerged Triumphant in Court," *New York Times*, February 21, 2022, *https://nyti.ms/3msXCpm*.

26 Cerberus Capital Management, LinkedIn profile, accessed August 2, 2022, *https://www.linkedin.com/company/cerberus-capital-management/*.

27 Kerry A. Dolan and Chase Peterson-Withorn, eds., "*Forbes* World's Billionaires List," *https://www.forbes.com/billionaires/*. As of August 2, 2022, Stephen Feinberg's net worth was $2.2 billion.

28 Science-Based Targets Initiative, *https://sciencebasedtargets.org/*.

29 "Global Thresholds and Allocations Council," r3.0, accessed July 29, 2022, *https://www.r3-0.org/gtac/*.

30 Bill Baue and Ralph Thurm, "r3.0 Public Comment Letter to I?SB: Nonsensical Definition/Definitional Cooptation and Sociopathic Materiality," r3.0, July 29, 2022, *https://r3dot0.medium.com/r3-0-public-comment-letter-to-i-sb-ae8ae5b4cc38*.

31 "What Is 'Double Materiality' and Why Should You Consider It?," Greenstone, August 25, 2021, *https://www.greenstoneplus.com/blog/what-is-double-materiality -and-why-should-you-consider-it*.

Chapter 10: The First Duty of Government Is to Protect Wealth

1   Frantz Fanon, *The Wretched of the Earth*, English ed. (New York: Grove Press, 1963, 2021), 1–2, 144. Citations refer to the 2021 edition.

2   The notable exception to monarchy was Indigenous societies, often more egalitarian in their governance. Among American Indians, well-known matrilineal societies include the Lenape, Hopi, Iroquois, and Chickasaw. Precolonial Africa was also characterized by the village community with collective ownership of land.

3   Quinn Slobodian, *Globalists: The End of Empire and the Birth of Neoliberalism* (Cambridge, MA, and London: Harvard University Press, 2018), 28, 107.

4   Slobodian, *Globalists*, 29.

5   Slobodian, *Globalists*, 14, 29, 33–34, 47, 115, 120, 124, 134.

6   Slobodian, *Globalists*, 28, 95, 112, 159.

7   Slobodian, *Globalists*, 144.

8   Slobodian, *Globalists*, 10, 16, 23, 116–118. Slobodian wrote that the "erstwhile Nazi jurist" Carl Schmitt in 1950 proposed that there was not one world but two; one was the world of the territorial state he termed *imperium*; the other was the world of property, which he termed *dominium*. Neoliberals felt he offered the best description of the world they wanted to conserve, with Ropke, Hayek, Robbins, and Mises all proposing a doubled world.

9   Slobodian, *Globalists*, 10, 29.

10 Slobodian, *Globalists*, 96–97. Moritz Bonn, an economist in the 1930s, wasn't a part of what would become the neoliberal movement. He spoke out against the errors of decolonization and government planning, speaking of the need for a borderless world economy of countercolonization, which he termed "invisible economic empire."

11 Slobodian, *Globalists*, 101.

12 Slobodian, *Globalists*, 116–117, 120, 125.

13 Slobodian, *Globalists*, 133.

14 Slobodian, *Globalists*, 125.

15 Between 2008 and 2015, the Federal Reserve balance sheet, its total assets, swelled from $900 billion to $4.5 trillion. Elizabeth Schulze, "The Fed Launched QE Nine Years Ago—These Four Charts Show Its Impact," CNBC, November 24, 2017, *https://cnb.cx/2POxHTj*; Chris Martin and Costas Milas,

"A Very Large Gamble: Evidence on Quantitative Easing in the US and UK," policy brief, Institute for Policy Research, University of Bath, n.d.

16 Justin Baltrusaitis, "Major Central Banks Pump $9 Trillion into the Economy amid Pandemic," Finbold, November 17, 2021, https://finbold.com/major -central-banks-pump-9-trillion-into-the-economy-amid-pandemic/. From early 2020 to November 2021, the world's four largest central banks—the US Federal Reserve, the European Central Bank, the Bank of Japan, and the Bank of England—used quantitative easing to inject more than $9 trillion into the global economy.

17 Maureen Groppe, "President Biden Signs $1.9 Trillion COVID-19 Relief Bill with $1,400 Stimulus Checks into Law," USA Today, March 11, 2021, https:// www.usatoday.com/story/news/politics/2021/03/11/joe-biden-signs-covid-19-re- lief-bill-stimulus-checks-into-law/4647894001/; "FACT SHEET: The American Rescue Plan Will Deliver Immediate Economic Relief to Families," US Department of the Treasury, March 18, 2021, https://home.treasury.gov/news/featured -stories/fact-sheet-the-american-rescue-plan-will-deliver-immediate-economic-relief -to-families.

18 Bill McKibben, "Congress Looks Set to Finally Pass Historic Climate Legislation," New Yorker, August 8, 2022, https://www.newyorker.com/magazine/2022 /08/08/congress-looks-set-to-finally-pass-historic-climate-legislation.

19 Mark Landler and Stephen Castle, "Truss, in Reversal, Drops Plan to Cut U.K. Tax Rate on High Earners," New York Times, October 3, 2022, https://nyti. ms/3Yyvxu4.

20 Frederic William Maitland, The Constitutional History of England: A Course of Lectures Delivered by F. W. Maitland, LL.D. (Cambridge, UK: The University Press, 1908); Cited in Charles A. Beard, An Economic Interpretation of the Constitution of the United States (New York: Macmillan, 1913; Old Tappan, NJ: The Free Press, 1986), 8 (footnote 1). Citations refer to the Free Press edition.

21 James Madison, Federalist Number 10, as discussed in Beard, An Economic Interpretation, 14–16. The rights of property originate from the "diversity in the faculties of men," Madison wrote. "The protection of these faculties is the first object of government." He added that "the most common and durable source of factions has been the various and unequal distribution of property," and that the regulation of these various interests "forms the principal task of modern legislation."

22 Beard, An Economic Interpretation, 64–67.

23 Removing selection of the president from direct vote and placing it in the hands of state-designated electors, the design of the Electoral College gave less populous slaveholding states disproportionate power—which they enjoyed in the Senate as well. James P. Pfiffner and Jason Hartke, "The Electoral College and the Framers' Distrust of Democracy," White House Studies 3, no. 3 (2003): 261–273.

24 James Madison, "Term of the Senate," June 26, 1787, Founders Online, National Archive, *https://founders.archives.gov/documents/Madison/01-10 -02-0044.*

Chapter 11: Extraction in the Extreme

1 Anthony Shorrocks, James Davies, and Rodrigo Lluberas, "Credit Suisse Research Institute Global Wealth Databook 2021," *https://www.credit-su- isse.com/media/assets/corporate/docs/about-us/research/publications/glob- al-wealth-databook-2021.pdf.* Reported in "Global Inequality," Inequality.org, accessed October 10, 2022, *https://inequality.org/facts/global-inequality/.*

2 "The World's Real-Time Billionaires," *Forbes,* reported in "Global Inequality," accessed October 10, 2022.

3 World Inequality Lab, "World Inequality Report 2022," reported in "Global Inequality," accessed October 10, 2022.

4 Dirk Bezemer, Michael Hudson, and Howard Reed, "Exploring the Capital Gains Economy: The Case of the UK," 2022 unpublished working paper commissioned by the Democracy Collaborative.

5 Author conversation with Dirk Bezemer, as part of staff dialogue at the Democracy Collaborative, November 16, 2022. The form in which the skimming off occurs, Bezemer noted, is in financial sector compensation. Workers in the financial sector were overpaid by as much as 50 percent in the precrisis years, based on their skills and the volatility of their income, according to Thomas Philippon and Ariell Reshef, "Wages and Human Capital in the U.S. Financial Industry: 1909–2006," National Bureau of Economic Research Working Paper No. w14644, January 2009, *https://ssrn.com/abstract=1329262.*

6 William Lazonick, Mustafa Erdem Sakinç, and Matt Hopkins, "Why Stock Buybacks Are Dangerous for the Economy," *Harvard Business Review,* January 7, 2020, *https://hbr.org/2020/01/why-stock-buybacks-are-dangerous-for-the- economy.* The 465 companies in the S&P 500 Index in January 2019 that were publicly listed between 2009 and 2018 spent, over that decade, $4.3 trillion in buybacks, equal to 52 percent of net income, and another $3.3 trillion on dividends, an additional 39 percent of net income.

7 This 2016 study found that the speculative US financial sector's excess profits, misallocation costs, and the 2008 financial crisis will have cost the US economy a cumulative $12.9 to $22.7 trillion between 1990 and 2023. Gerald Epstein and Juan Antonio Montecino, *Overcharged: The High Cost of High Finance* (New York: Roosevelt Institute, 2016).

8 "Misery Index," *Jacobin* 46 (Summer 2022): 151.

9 The analysis of these various damages from financialization draws from Beze- mer et al., "Exploring"; Michael Hudson and Dirk Bezemer, "Rent-Seeking and Asset Price Inflation: A Total Returns Profile of Economic Polarization in America," *Review of Keynesian Economics* 9, no. 4 (October 2021); Delilah

Rothenberg, Raphaele Chappe, and Amanda Feldman, "ESG 2.0: Measuring and Managing Investor Risks Beyond the Enterprise-Level," April 6, 2021, *https://ssrn.com/abstract=3820316*; and Nicholas Shaxson, *The Finance Curse* (New York: Grove Press, 2019).

10 Jeremy Corbyn has been discredited. Yet in 2015, he was elected leader of the British Labour party in a stunning victory, winning nearly 60 percent of first-preference votes. It was young people who swept him to victory, and he said the message was that people are "fed up with the injustice and the inequality" of Britain. As the *Guardian* wrote, Corbyn was one of the most left-wing, anti-establishment leaders ever chosen. Rowena Mason, "Labour Leadership: Jeremy Corbyn Elected with Huge Mandate," *Guardian*, September 12, 2015, *https://www.theguardian.com/politics/2015/sep/12/jeremy-corbyn-wins-labour-party-leadership-election*.

Chapter 12: A Society Half Plutocratic, Half Democratic

1 On November 18, 2020, 70 percent of Republicans said Biden won only due to voter fraud. Philip Bump, "Nearly 700 Days Later, Most Republicans Still Believe Trump's Big Lie," *Washington Post*, September 28, 2022, *https://wapo.st/3Yx2veu*.

2 Karen Yourisk et al., "2020 Election Skeptics Crowd the Republican Ticket Nationwide," *New York Times*, October 15, 2022, *https://nyti.ms/3F8Y82n*.

3 Jane Mayer, "The Big Money Behind the Big Lie," *New Yorker*, August 9, 2021, *https://www.newyorker.com/magazine/2021/08/09/the-big-money-behind-the-big-lie*.

4 Mayer, "Big Money," 32.

5 "State-Level Republicans Are 'Reforming' How Elections Are Administered," *Economist*, July 3, 2021, *https://econ.st/3J5yQDD*.

6 Jane Mayer, *Dark Money* (New York: Anchor Books, 2017), xvii.

7 Mayer, "Big Money," 33.

8 W. E. B. Du Bois, *Black Reconstruction in America, 1860–1880* (New York: Harcourt, Brace & Howe, 1935).

9 Jacob S. Hacker and Paul Pierson, *Let Them Eat Tweets: How the Right Rules in an Age of Extreme Inequality* (New York: Liveright Publishing, 2020), 1–10.

10 Mayer, *Dark Money*, xviii, xxii.

11 Senator Sheldon Whitehouse, *Captured: The Corporate Infiltration of American Democracy* (New York, London: The New Press, 2017), xvii–xix.

12 Nick Corbishley, "European Systemic Risk Board Issues First Ever 'General Warning' About 'Financial Stability Risks,'" Naked Capitalism, September 30, 2022, *https://www.nakedcapitalism.com/2022/09/european-systemic-risk-board-just-issued-its-first-ever-general-warning-about-rising-risks-in-europes-financial-system.html*.

13 Richard Partington, "IMF Chief Warns World Heading Towards Age of Greater Instability," *Guardian*, October 6, 2022, *https://www.theguardian.com*

/business/2022/oct/06/imf-chief-warns-world-is-heading-towards-an-age-of
-breakdown.

14 Michael Hudson and Dirk Bezemer, "Rent-Seeking and Asset Price Inflation: A
Total Returns Profile of Economic Polarization in America," *Review of Keynesian Economics* 9, no. 4 (October 2021).

15 The S&P 500 hit a closing low of 677 on March 9, 2009. It closed at 4,791 on
December 27, 2021 (4,791 divided by 677 equals slightly more than 7). "S&P
500," Yahoo! Finance, accessed December 2, 2022, https://yhoo.it/3LcXa94.

16 This concept and much of the language first appeared in an internal 2019
Democracy Collaborative strategy document, "Back from the Brink," by Marjorie Kelly and Joe Guinan. Joe used some of this language in his piece with Sarah
McKinley, "Hanging in the Balance: The Democratic Economy after Corbyn,"
Renewal 28, no. 1 (Spring 2020).

Part III: Where We Begin

1 "What Is U.S. Electricity Generation by Generation Source?," US Energy
Information Administration, accessed March 8, 2023, https://www.eia.gov/tools
/faqs/faq.php?id=427&t=3.

Chapter 13: Breaking the Trance

1 David Gelles, "Billionaire No More: Patagonia Founder Gives Away the Company," *New York Times*, September 14, 2022, https://nyti.ms/3ZTWbPa.

2 Donella Meadows, "Leverage Points: Places to Intervene in a System," The
Donella Meadows Project: Academy for Systems Change, accessed March 8,
2023, https://donellameadows.org/archives/leverage-points-places-to-intervene
-in-a-system/.

3 John Steinbeck, *The Grapes of Wrath* (New York: Viking Press, 1939; Dorset
Press, 1976), 42, 44. Citations refer to the Dorset Press edition.

4 Meadows, "Leverage Points."

5 Mark Fisher, *Capitalist Realism* (Winchester, UK, and Washington, DC: Zero
Books, 2009), 6, 14, 78.

6 Fisher, *Capitalist Realism*, 21.

7 Fisher, *Capitalist Realism*, 15.

8 Fisher, *Capitalist Realism*, 63.

Chapter 14: Pranks, New Naming, and Other Subversive Acts

1 Nathan Schneider, "Here's My Plan to Save Twitter: Let's Buy It," *Guardian*,
September 29, 2016, https://www.theguardian.com/commentisfree/2016/
sep/29/save-twitter-buy-platform-shared-ownership.

2   Danny Spitzberg, "Cooperative Organizing for an Inclusive Economy: The Campaign to #BuyTwitter," *NCBA [National Cooperative Business Association] Journal* (Summer 2017).

3   Author interview with Danny Spitzberg, December 13, 2022.

4   Spitzberg, "Cooperative Organizing."

5   Author interview and email correspondence with Danny Spitzberg, December 13, 2022; January 25, 2023. Danny Spitzberg and Nathan Schneider, "You— Yes, You!—Would Be a Better Owner for Twitter than Elon Musk," *Wired*, April 16, 2022, *https://www.wired.com/story/you-yes-you-would-be-a-better -owner-for-twitter-than-elon-musk/*.

6   Bill Baue and Ralph Thurm, "r3.0 Public Comment Letter to I?SB: Nonsensical Definition/Definitional Cooptation and Sociopathic Materiality," r3.0, July 29, 2022, *https://r3dot0.medium.com/r3-0-public-comment-letter-to-i-sb-ae8ae5b4cc38*.

7   E. F. Schumacher, "Buddhist Economics," in *Small Is Beautiful: Economics as If People Mattered* (London: Blond & Briggs, 1973; Vancouver, BC: Hartley & Marks Publishers, 1999), 43. Citation refers to Hartley & Marks edition.

8   Author conversation with Dirk Bezemer, part of staff dialogue at the Democracy Collaborative, November 16, 2022.

9   Marjorie Kelly, "Lords of the Earth," in *The Divine Right of Capital* (San Francisco: Berrett-Koehler Publishers, 2001). I note there (page 35) the observation by Adolf Berle, coauthor of *The Modern Corporation and Private Property*, who wrote in its 1967 edition, "Stock markets are no longer places of 'investment.'... [They are] only psychologically connected with the capital gathering and capital application system on which productive industry and enterprise actually depend."

10 National Center for Employee Ownership, Service Provider Directory, *https:// www.nceo.org/service-provider-directory*.

11 "Contingent Workforce: Size, Characteristics, Earnings, and Benefits," US Government Accountability Office, April 20, 2015, *https://www.gao.gov/products /gao-15-168r*.

12 Dirk Bezemer, Michael Hudson, and Howard Reed, "Exploring the Capital Gains Economy: The Case of the UK," 2022 unpublished working paper commissioned by the Democracy Collaborative.

13 Author correspondence with Dirk Bezemer, January 17, 2023.

14 Remark by Michael Hudson at staff gathering by the Democracy Collaborative, November 16, 2022.

15 Remarks by Neva Goodwin at the Democracy Collaborative gathering on next system capital, July 19, 2022; correspondence with author, January 20–21, 2023.

16 Edward Said, *Culture and Imperialism*, New York: Vintage/Random House, 1994, xii.

Chapter 15: The Democratic Economy

1   Marjorie Kelly and Ted Howard, *The Making of a Democratic Economy* (San Francisco: Berrett-Koehler Publishers, 2019), 3.

2 Amartya Sen, *Development as Freedom* (New York: Knopf, 1999).

3 Martha Nussbaum, *Frontiers of Justice: Disability, Nationality, Species Member-ship* (Cambridge, MA, and London: Belknap Press), 2006, 76–78, 108–113, 325–328.

4 Gabriel Poblete, "How NYC's Right to Shelter Mandate Works," *City and State*, October 7, 2021, *https://www.cityandstateny.com/policy/2021/10/how-nycs -right-shelter-mandate-works/185933/*.

5 Anupreeta Dass, Emily Flitter, and Nicholas Kulish, "A Culture of Fear at the Firm That Manages Bill Gates's Fortune," *New York Times*, May 26, 2021, *https://nyti.ms/3IZSDEl*.

6 Emily Thaden and Greg Rosenberg, "Outperforming the Market: Delinquency and Foreclosure Rates in Community Land Trusts," Lincoln Institute of Land Policy, *Land Lines* (October 2010).

7 Alexandra Applegate, "Community Land Trusts Are Building Disaster-Resilient Neighborhoods," Next City, November 10, 2022, *https://nextcity.org /urbanist-news/community-land-trusts-are-building-disaster-resilient-neighborhoods*.

8 Oscar Perry Abello, "Philly's Kensington Corridor Is Taking Back Power Over Economic Development," Next City, February 25, 2021, *https://nextcity.org/ urbanist-news/phillys-kensington-corridor-is-taking-back-power-over-economic -development*.

9 Scotty Hendricks, "What Are Municipal Utilities and Why Are They Suddenly Popular?," Big Think, November 26, 2019, *https://bigthink.com/the-present /municipal-electricity-utility/*.

12 National Credit Union Administration Quarterly Credit Union Data Summary 2022 Q3, ii, *https://ncua.gov/files/publications/analysis/quarterly-data-summary -2022-Q3.pdf*.

11 Kelsey MacKinnon, "Paving the Way for Rideshare Cooperatives," OnLabor, May 18, 2022, *https://onlabor.org/paving-the-way-for-rideshare-cooperatives/*.

12 Privately held companies with ESOPs in 2019 numbered 5,880, with 2 million participants and total plan assets of $203 billion. These companies tend to be majority owned by workers. "Employee Ownership by the Numbers," National Center for Employee Ownership, December 2021, *https://www.nceo.org/articles /employee-ownership-by-the-numbers*.

13 See, for example, "Doughnut Economics in the Deep Design of Business," May 18, 2022, *https://doughnuteconomics.org/news/50*.

14 "PBC Company—Definition of Public Benefit Corporation & Compare PBC vs B Corp vs Nonprofits," accessed January 26, 2023, *https://buildd.co/funding /public-benefit-corporation*.

15 Elizabeth Warren, "Companies Shouldn't Be Accountable Only to Shareholders," *Wall Street Journal*, August 14, 2018, *https://on.wsj.com/2nERRDl*.

16 Marjorie Kelly, "The End of the Corporation?" Transnational Institute, January 18, 2020, *https://longreads.tni.org/stateofpower/the-end-of-the-corporation*.

17 Abe Bortz, "Old Age Pensions: A Brief History," Social Welfare History Project, Virginia Commonwealth University, accessed March 8, 2023, *https://socialwelfare.library.vcu.edu/issues/old-age/old-age-pensions-a-brief-history/*; "Fact Sheet: Social Security," US Social Security Administration, June 2022 data, accessed January 3, 2022, *https://www.ssa.gov/OACT/FACTS/*.

Chapter 16: Democratizing Finance

1 Remarks via Zoom by Herman Daly, Tellus Institute, Cambridge, MA, February 3, 2022.

2 Gary Snyder, *The Practice of the Wild* (Berkeley, CA: Counterpoint, 1990).

3 Bill McKibben, "Congress Looks Set to Finally Pass Historic Climate Legislation," *New Yorker*, August 8, 2022, *https://www.newyorker.com/magazine/2022/08/08/congress-looks-set-to-finally-pass-historic-climate-legislation*.

4 On the falseness of the old narrative, see, for example, Bill McKibben, "In a World on Fire, Stop Burning Things," *New Yorker*, March 18, 2022, *https://www.newyorker.com/news/essay/in-a-world-on-fire-stop-burning-things*.

5 Fred Block and Robert Hockett, eds., *The Real Utopias Project: Democratizing Finance: Transforming Credit to Transform Society* (London, New York: Verso, 2022).

6 Lucian Bebchuk and Jessie Fried, "Executive Compensation at Fannie Mae: A Case Study of Perverse Incentives, Nonperformance Pay, and Camouflage," *Journal of Corporation Law* 30, no. 4 (2005): 807–822, *https://ssrn.com/abstract=653125*.

7 Jack Moriarty, ed., "Turning Employees Into Owners: Rebuilding the American Dream," Ownership America, Fall 2021, *https://ownershipamerica.org/publications/*.

8 Block and Hockett, *The Real Utopias*.

9 "Green Liberty Bonds $25 Million Second Issuance Sells Out," Connecticut Green Bank, April 23, 2021, *https://www.ctgreenbank.com/green-liberty-bonds-2nd-issuance-sells-out/*.

10 "Restorative Economics: Creating Community Benefits by Shifting Who Owns and Controls Assets," in the *ImpactAlpha* podcast, October 24, 2021, *https://impactalpha.com/restorative-economics-creating-community-benefits-by-shifting-who-owns-and-controls-assets-podcast/*.

11 Michael Hudson, "A Debt Jubilee Is the Only Way to Avoid a Depression," *Washington Post*, March 21, 2020, *https://wapo.st/3J3USGx*.

12 Nicholas Owen, "Belize: Swapping Debt for Nature," International Monetary Fund, May 4, 2022, *https://www.imf.org/en/News/Articles/2022/05/03/CF-Belize-swapping-debt-for-nature*.

13 Hudson, "Debt Jubilee."

14 Yuki Noguchi, "The Group's Wiped Out $6.7 Billion in Medical Debt, and It's Just Getting Started," NPR, August 15, 2022, *https://n.pr/3J2g3Jd*; Elizabeth

Bruenig, "Forgive Us Our Debts," *New York Times*, November 23, 2020, *https://nyti.ms/3JnZE34*.

15 Bruenig, "Forgive Us."

16 Emma Bubola, "This Heir to a Fortune Wants It Taken Away for Fairness' Sake," *New York Times*, October 22, 2022, *https://nyti.ms/3JrZyrt*.

17 Shira Markoff et al., "A Brighter Future with Baby Bonds: How States and Cities Should Invest in Our Kids," Prosperity Now and the New School's Institute on Race, Power and Political Economy, January 2022, *https://prosperitynow.org/statebabybonds*.

18 "New Climate Risks Scorecard Outlines Clear Demands of the Private Equity Industry," Private Equity Stakeholder Project, October 4, 2022, *https://pestakeholder.org/news/new-climate-risks-scorecard-outlines-clear-demands-of-the-private-equity-industry/*.

19 Delilah Rothenberg, Raphaele Chappe, and Amanda Feldman, "ESG 2.0: Measuring and Managing Investor Risks Beyond the Enterprise-Level," April 6, 2021, *https://ssrn.com/abstract=3820316*.

Chapter 17: Beginning Where You Live

1 Sarah McKinley, "All Things Being Unequal," *The Mint*, December 18, 2022, *https://www.themintmagazine.com/all-things-being-unequal/*.

2 Comment by Neil McInroy on the *Laura Flanders Show* (podcast), "Community Wealth Building: An Economic Reset," June 10, 2022, *https://lauraflanders.org/2022/06/community-wealth-building/*.

3 Author dialogue with Neil McInroy, January 20, 2023.

4 "Community Wealth Building Initiative," City of Chicago, *https://www.chicago.gov/city/en/sites/community-wealth-building/home.html*.

5 Sarah McKinley and Neil McInroy, "Chicago, Scotland Take a Community Wealth Building Approach to Economic Development," *The Hill*, October 31, 2022, *https://thehill.com/opinion/congress-blog/3713186-chicago-scotland-take-a-community-wealth-building-approach-to-economic-development/*.

6 "Implementing Community Wealth Building: A Guide," Economic Development Association Scotland and CLES, January 2013, *https://edas.org.uk/community-wealth-building-guide/*.

7 "Community Wealth Building," North Ayrshire Council, accessed January 20, 2023, *https://www.north-ayrshire.gov.uk/council/community-wealth-building/community-wealth-building.aspx*.

8 McKinley and McInroy, "Chicago, Scotland."

9 "Auchrannie Becomes Scotland's First Employee-Owned Resort," BBC News, January 9, 2018, *https://bbc.in/3FbDGOl*.

10 Jessica Rose and Marjorie Kelly, with Sarah Stranahan, Michelle Camou and Karen Kahn, "Opportunity Knocking: Impact Capital as the Transformative Agent to Take Employee Ownership to Scale," Democracy Collaborative,

January 2021, *https://thedemocracycollaborative.com/learn/publication/opportunity-knocking-impact-capital-transformative-agent-take-employee-ownership.*

11 Karen Kahn, "Apis & Heritage Brings Justice Lens to ESOP Transitions," Democracy Collaborative, June 28, 2022, *https://www.fiftybyfifty.org/2022/06/apis-heritage-brings-justice-lens-to-esop-transitions/.*

12 Richard May, Robert Hockett, and Christopher Mackin, "Encouraging Inclusive Growth: The Employee Equity Loan Act," *Challenge* 62, no. 6 (October 2019): 377–397.

13 In 1995, there were 9,232 plans covering 7.2 million workers. Today, there are 6,482 ESOPs covering 10.2 million active members. "Employee Ownership by the Numbers," National Center for Employee Ownership, accessed March 8, 2023, *https://www.nceo.org/articles/employee-ownership-by-the-numbers.*

14 "The History and Composition of ESOPs," PCE Investment Bankers, Inc., accessed March 8, 2023, *https://www.pcecompanies.com/resources/the-history-and-composition-of-esops.*

15 Background on Employee Equity Investment Act prepared by office of Rep. Dean Phillips, 2022.

16 Author dialogue with Mary, who asked that her last name not be used, February 22, 2023, and March 6, 2023.

Conclusion: We're Not Talking About the Real Problem Yet

1 "The median return at US colleges for the last fiscal year was 27% and 34% for endowments with more than $500 million of assets." Mike Scutari, "University Endowments Have Grown Dramatically. How Should Officials Allocate the Earnings?," *Inside Philanthropy,* January 13, 2022, *https://www.insidephilanthropy.com/home/2022/1/13/university-endowments-have-grown-dramatically-how-should-officials-allocate-the-earnings.*

Resources for Action

Companies and Business Schools

Every kind and size of company, globally, can elect to become a B Corporation, or in the US can incorporate in most states as a benefit corporation. Both these actions mean embracing in governing documents a commitment to serving many stakeholders. Even publicly traded companies are beginning to take such steps. Many companies use employee ownership of various kinds. Some firms are undertaking comprehensive redesign initiatives to rethink their ownership design. Business school faculty and students are also engaged.

- If your organization is considering forming a committee to explore becoming a B Corporation or benefit corporation, learn more at *https://www.bcorporation.net*.

- If your business or business school is interested in ownership redesign, explore the Doughnut Design Tool for Business created by the Doughnut Economy Action Lab (founded by economist Kate Raworth, author of *Doughnut Economics*). A doughnut economy is one that stays within planetary boundaries and societal boundaries of well-being. This tool is being used by business schools and companies across the world: *https://doughnuteconomics.org/tools/191*.

- If your firm is considering adding employee ownership, you'll find helpful materials from the National Center for Employee Ownership (NCEO): *https://www.nceo.org/*.

- If a company division will be spun off and managers might be interested in leading a worker buyout, you can find an ESOP expert through NCEO's Service Provider Directory: *https:// www.nceo.org/service-provider-directory.*

Community Wealth Building

- If your community is considering doing an inventory of community wealth building (CWB) institutions, you can learn more at the Democracy Collaborative site: *https://democracy collaborative.org/programs/cwb.*

- Anchors are large nonprofits rooted in place, like universities, museums, and nonprofit hospital systems, as well as city governments and schools. The Evergreen Cooperatives in Cleveland were supported by local anchors, including the Cleveland Clinic, which uses the worker-owned Evergreen Cooperative Laundry as its primary laundry vendor. More than seventy health systems are members of the Healthcare Anchor Network, together sharing how to use their purchasing, hiring, and investing to benefit the health and well-being of their communities: *https://healthcareanchor.network/.*

- There are two thousand publicly owned and eight hundred cooperatively owned electric utilities in the US. To check for your town or city, see the map at the American Public Power Association: *https://www.publicpower.org/where-public-power.*

- To find out how many worker-owned firms are in your community, consult the Certified Employee Owned directory, which lists more than six thousand US companies with significant, broad-based employee ownership: *https://www.certifiedeo .com/companies.* Find worker co-ops through the US Federation of Worker Cooperatives and the Democracy at Work Institute directory: *https://www.usworker.coop/directory/.*

- To learn if your state has a center for employee ownership, check the Employee Ownership Expansion Network: *https://www.eoxnetwork.org/state-centers.*

- Land banks are government or nonprofit entities that assemble, own, and manage vacant or foreclosed property in order to stabilize neighborhoods and encourage responsible redevelopment. To find out if your community has one, consult the national map of land banks at *https://communityprogress.org/resources/land-banks/national-land-bank-map/.*

- Learn more about community land trusts, which create permanently affordable home ownership for generations of lower-income families (as discussed in chapter 15), through the Grounded Solutions Network at *https://groundedsolutions.org/strengthening-neighborhoods/community-land-trusts.*

- Find community development financial institutions (CDFIs) in your area through the Opportunity Finance Network's directory at *https://www.ofn.org/cdfi-locator/.*

- In the US and Canada, the Land Back movement advocates reestablishing political and economic control over the ancestral land of Indigenous communities. Learn more at *https://landback.org/.*

- Perpetual purpose trusts, referenced in chapters 13 and 15, create community benefit through shared ownership for businesses, real estate, land, and more. Purpose US is an arm of the international nonprofit advancing this model, working, for example, with groups in Philadelphia; Kansas City, Missouri; Tulsa, Oklahoma; and Atlanta on trusts that remove real estate from the speculative market and put it under community-controlled governance. See *https://www.purpose-us.com/.*

Next System of Capital

- If you or institutions you're connected to—your church, college, city and state pension funds—are interested in exploring local investing and impact investing, get started by reading Michael Shuman's *Put Your Money Where Your Life Is* or sign up for his free Main Street Journal at *https://www.themainstreetjournal.org/*. Learn about impact investing through the Global Impact Investing Network at *https://thegiin.org/*.

- As the debtors' union US Debt Collective says, "Alone our debts are a burden. Together they make us powerful." If you're interested in understanding how to cancel unjust debt, explore this organization at *https://debtcollective.org/*. In the UK, explore Debt Justice at *https://debtjustice.org.uk/*.

- To learn about forgiving medical debt for pennies on the dollar, as discussed in chapter 16, explore the nonprofit RIP Medical Debt at *https://ripmedicaldebt.org/*.

- Check out the Private Equity Stakeholder Project, which engages with communities and families impacted by private equity: *https://pestakeholder.org/*.

- If you're interested in big ideas about a next system of capital, like Robert Hockett's idea of turning the Federal Reserve into a people's Fed, read *Democratizing Finance: Restructuring Credit to Transform Society*, part of the Real Utopias Project, edited by Fred Block and Robert Hockett (London/New York: Verso, 2022).

- To better understand financialization, a good place to start is Nicholas Shaxson's book *The Finance Curse* (New York: Grove Press, 2018).

Acknowledgments

AS THIS BOOK IS the culmination of more than thirty years of my professional work, there are more people to whom I owe a debt of gratitude than can possibly be mentioned here. First I want to acknowledge and honor my sister Valerie Kelly, to whom this book is dedicated, who has always been there for me in more ways than I can count; I could not be who I am without Valerie. My wife, Shelley Alpern, has been of incalculable support and help (and joy); our path together began at a socially responsible investing conference where we met, and she brought her sharp eye both for investing and for language to her close editing of this book, honing the arguments, saving me from missteps, adding welcome humor (in chapter 14, Acme and Wile E. Coyote were Shelley's additions). I am enormously grateful to my fact checker, Will Flagle, for being my safety net and parachute. Any errors that remain are my own.

Steve Piersanti of Berrett-Koehler, whom I've known now for thirty years and with whom I've published all my books, gave this work the most careful attention I've ever received from an editor, improving and polishing and clarifying its message. All the people of Berrett-Koehler have been wonderful to work with, including Jeevan Sivasubramaniam, Mike Crowley, Rachel Monaghan, Maureen Forys, and Ashley Ingram. I'd like to give a special shout-out to Maria Jesus Aguilo for coming up with the final name for this book.

Many thanks to Leslie Harroun, Amy Gluckman, and Karen Kahn for helping develop and carry out the July meeting about next system capital; working with them made it more effective and far more fun. I am particularly grateful to Pratistha Joshi Rajkarnikar and her colleagues at the Economics in Context Initiative at the Global Development Policy Center, Boston University, for generously hosting the meeting. Special thanks to all the participants in that meeting for giving so generously of their time and ideas: Dana Brown, Mark Campanale, Grieve Chelwa, Leslie Christian, Neva Goodwin, Joe Guinan, Pamela Icyeza, Stephanie McHenry, Delilah Rothenberg, Michael Shuman, and Evan Steiner.

The early readers of a first draft of this book deserve a special nod and thank you for their reactions and feedback, which helped shape this into a more finished work: Britt Bravo, David Dearth, Mary Emeny, Amy Gluckman, Jennifer Hall, and Johann Klaassen. Reacting to the notion of wealth supremacy and capital bias as the DNA of the system, Jen in particular added the colorful notion that these entwined strands of bias define how the system talks, walks, grows limbs, expands, and regenerates itself. Special thanks to Amy, a former editor at *Dollars and Sense*, who offered many thoughtful edits from her close read of the manuscript, as well as delightful dialogue over many of the ideas.

For insight into the central notion of financialization, so critical to understanding the impact of the extractive system, I am deeply indebted to Dirk Bezemer, Michael Hudson, and Howard Reed; read chapters 7 and 11 in particular, which draw on their work, and you will never see the world the same way again.

Many thanks also to those I interviewed and who allowed their stories to be told and their comments to be quoted in this book, including Mandy Cabot, Kate Emery, Neil McInroy, Gideon Rosen-blatt, and Danny Spitzberg, with double thanks to Leslie Christian and Neva Goodwin, who are quoted elsewhere in the book in addition to participating in the July meeting.

I will always hold deep gratitude to Ted Howard, cofounder of the Democracy Collaborative (TDC), for making our work together possible and for supporting me in writing this book; the book Ted and I did together, *The Making of a Democratic Economy*, laid the ground-work for this one. Special thanks to Joe Guinan, president of TDC, who long encouraged me to write about the concept of capital bias, and to Stephanie McHenry, CEO of TDC, for her support and part-nership with the July meeting and in all the work she does to hold the TDC family together.

Index

About the Author

MARJORIE KELLY is distinguished senior fellow at the Democracy Collaborative (TDC), a research and development lab for the democratic economy that develops and implements transformative economic solutions. She is a recognized expert in enterprise and financial design for social mission. Marjorie's first book, *The Divine Right of Capital*, inspired the creation of the B Corporation movement, according to the cofounder of that movement, Jay Coen Gilbert.

Marjorie comes from a business family, where her father owned a small business and her grandfather founded Anderson Tool and Die in Chicago. She has been a social activist since her time as an English student at Earlham College, where she protested the Vietnam War. During her time pursuing a master's in journalism at the University of Missouri, her real political awakening occurred, as she discovered feminism and came out as a lesbian. That was an early exercise in questioning received wisdom and recognizing invisible bias, which has deeply shaped her life's work, particularly this book on wealth supremacy.

Perceiving that business is the most powerful force on the planet, Marjorie cofounded *Business Ethics* magazine in 1987 to work for

social change by supporting the young movement for socially responsible business and investing. She believed then that good businesspeople could change the world. But as she saw social mission squeezed
out in company after company, after those firms went public or sold
to multinationals, she recognized that the problem is systemic. She
wrote her first book, *The Divine Right of Capital*, to explain how the
systemic bias toward capital shapes corporations. Published in 2001,
that book is still used in MBA classes today; it was named one of the
ten best business books of the year by *Library Journal* and won Marjorie induction into the honorary portrait gallery of "Americans Who
Tell the Truth." Her other books, *Owning Our Future* and *The Making
of the Democratic Economy*, point toward solutions in the design of
ownership and the broader models of a democratic economy.

Marjorie publishes and speaks widely. She has been a longtime
student of Buddhism, studying for years under Steve Hagen of
Dharma Field Zen Center in Minneapolis. In her previous work at
Tellus Institute, and now at the Democracy Collaborative, she has
consulted broadly. Her projects have included the Ford Foundation's
WealthWorks initiative, developing innovations in rural development
in the Deep South and Appalachia; TDC's work with Native American leaders on Pine Ridge and elsewhere; aiding community foundations with place-based impact investing; and cofounding the Fifty by
Fifty project at TDC to advance worker ownership. She lives in the
Boston area with her wife, Shelley Alpern.

Berrett–Koehler
Publishers

Berrett-Koehler is an independent publisher dedicated to an ambitious mission: *Connecting people and ideas to create a world that works for all.*

Our publications span many formats, including print, digital, audio, and video. We also offer online resources, training, and gatherings. And we will continue expanding our products and services to advance our mission.

We believe that the solutions to the world's problems will come from all of us, working at all levels: in our society, in our organizations, and in our own lives. Our publications and resources offer pathways to creating a more just, equitable, and sustainable society. They help people make their organizations more humane, democratic, diverse, and effective (and we don't think there's any contradiction there). And they guide people in creating positive change in their own lives and aligning their personal practices with their aspirations for a better world.

And we strive to practice what we preach through what we call "The BK Way." At the core of this approach is *stewardship,* a deep sense of responsibility to administer the company for the benefit of all of our stakeholder groups, including authors, customers, employees, investors, service providers, sales partners, and the communities and environment around us. Everything we do is built around stewardship and our other core values of *quality, partnership, inclusion,* and *sustainability.*

This is why Berrett-Koehler is the first book publishing company to be both a B Corporation (a rigorous certification) and a benefit corporation (a for-profit legal status), which together require us to adhere to the highest standards for corporate, social, and environmental performance. And it is why we have instituted many pioneering practices (which you can learn about at www.bkconnection.com), including the Berrett-Koehler Constitution, the Bill of Rights and Responsibilities for BK Authors, and our unique Author Days.

We are grateful to our readers, authors, and other friends who are supporting our mission. We ask you to share with us examples of how BK publications and resources are making a difference in your lives, organizations, and communities at www.bkconnection.com/impact.

Dear reader,

Thank you for picking up this book and welcome to the worldwide BK community! You're joining a special group of people who have come together to create positive change in their lives, organizations, and communities.

What's BK all about?

Our mission is to connect people and ideas to create a world that works for all.

Why? Our communities, organizations, and lives get bogged down by old paradigms of self-interest, exclusion, hierarchy, and privilege. But we believe that can change. That's why we seek the leading experts on these challenges—and share their actionable ideas with you.

A welcome gift

To help you get started, we'd like to offer you a **free copy** of one of our bestselling ebooks:

www.bkconnection.com/welcome

When you claim your **free ebook**, you'll also be subscribed to our blog.

Our freshest insights

Access the best new tools and ideas for leaders at all levels on our blog at ideas.bkconnection.com.

Sincerely,

Your friends at Berrett-Koehler

MIX
Paper from responsible sources
FSC® C016245

Certified

Corporation